Grief Sucks; But Hope Again

A Memoir of Loss and Pain

Brilliant Pongo

Published by Brilliant Pongo
Publishing partner: Paragon Publishing, Rothersthorpe
First published 2022

ISBN 978-1-78222-934-6

Book design, layout and production management by Into Print
www.intoprint.net
+44 (0)1604 832149

Preface

Grieving, surely sucks
When do you start; when do you end?

It took me over two years to get to a place or state of mind in which I could comfortably communicate my experience with grief and the loss of my wife.

Indeed, grief is complex; it may present itself differently on any given day. It is my desire that as I narrate my account and journey of grief and grieving with a collection of my reflections, poems, and musings, someone out there will benefit from my story. I will speak about topics like loneliness, grief attacks, hope, love, and creating meaning as I learnt to live fully with my grief.

The loss of a loved one can be among one of the most overwhelming and painful experiences you are likely to encounter. It comes uninvited and it takes you through a range of emotions which often contradict one another and make no sense.

Grief, can you leave you feeling a whirlwind of emotions. It is a difficult process in many ways. It is in itself a hard emotion, problematic to explain. Grief can be difficult and stressful and nearly everybody goes through it at some point in their lives. Despite this, it can be very difficult to predict how we might react to a loss, as it is a very individual process.

The physical pain of it can have a negative effect on your health and may alter your behaviour, and disturb your sleeping, eating, and thinking.

The emotions caused by the loss of a loved one can be difficult to manage and understandably they can be difficult to face. However, it is important that you face up to these grief-caused emotions and walk through the processes rather than avoid or suppress them. Because they can end up impacting your life in many ways, hurting yourself and others.

People grieve in different ways. Cultural and societal differences influence the way in which we grieve.

We go through a variety of emotional experiences such as anger, confusion, and sadness. There is no right or wrong way to feel following a loss. Some people seek help immediately by showing their emotions and talking to people, others prefer to deal with things slowly, quietly or by themselves.

A theory developed by psychiatrist Elisabeth Kübler-Ross suggests that we go through five distinct stages of grief after the loss of a loved one: denial, anger, bargaining, depression, and acceptance. I personally don't think there is a particular order on how individuals grieve and so I will tell my story.

Walk with me as I narrate my grief-journey.

Dedication:

I dedicate this book to a special woman who helped shape me into the man that I am today.

Tshidz was a strong woman.

Speaking about Tshidz through my most difficult moments of my grieving brought me a feeling of comfort and longing. She was strong woman a very assertive individual with a bubbly personality. She was straightforward about her wants and needs. Tshidz often rubbed people the wrong way. However, she was a woman who was strong and at times complex. She had a background that had created the need to be gritty, tenacious, and passionate in a way that other people might have taken offence to.

Many of our friends and those she encountered might have interpreted her character as demanding or even bossy. But the truth is she was a strong woman who was very sensitive and thoughtful.

She stood up for herself. She was outspoken when it came to confronting others about being treated poorly. When an injustice took place, she spoke up rather than let it roll off.

She invested in herself. Whether it was learning something new, pushing herself to be healthier, or taking a big step outside her comfort zone, she knew that the investments she made for herself, and her life offered guaranteed dividends.

She had boundaries. When she made a decision, she checked in with herself first to see if she really wants to do it and has the time and space to invest in an opportunity. She said yes to opportunities which strengthened hers and no to those that diminish her position.

She celebrated other women. As a strong woman that she was she encouraged other women. She focused on recognising and celebrating the strengths that she saw in other women. She was vocal in her support.

She knew her worth. While she didn't always feel beautiful, intelligent, charming, interesting, or even strong, she knew that she always brought value. Whenever she found herself in a situation with someone who devalues her, she would either make it known or leave at the first opportunity.

She never relied on others' opinions about her life. She might have internalised negativity; she always made an effort to let the negative comments pass and didn't allow the remarks of others to stop her from what is right for her. She understood that negativity says more about the person flinging it than it does about her.

She was confident. Tshidz had a well-defined sense of identity, and her actions were in line with her morals and beliefs. Tshidz did not have a need to win others over. She stayed true to her own beliefs.

I know that for Tshidz being a strong woman was a choice she made. But like most of us she experienced fear, anxiety, insecurity, and other negative emotions that can tear us down. Nonetheless she chose to commit to herself. She truly embraced the idea that she would never give anything, or anyone, the power to break her.

Tshidz was passionate about empowering other women. She set up an organisation called Girl Code101 which aimed to do just that. Tshidz was a strong woman who could walk into a room and hold her own with class, grace, and style. For her it was never about being rude or demanding. Rather, it was more about maintaining a personal commitment to guide herself through difficult situations.

I'm proud to say she was "too much." I'm proud to say she was strong. That was my Tshidz, and I dedicate this book to her loving memory.

Introduction

Losing someone close to you – whether that's because of a death in the family, a divorce, or the ending of a friendship – is hard. Along with the initial shock, it's a challenge but my experiences on this grieving journey have taught me that no matter how tough things get one must go on and learn how to navigate the future without them by your side.

My wife Tshidz was a very affectionate and sociable person. I remember the very first day I met her – she sat on the stairway to my office, strangely she had a full loaf of bread and for some reason best known to her she tore away at this loaf munching it away as if no one was watching her.

I was blown away by her character I knew then that she was different, and I wanted her as my friend, I wanted her as my partner and as my wife. We instantly connected and two years later we got married.

My wife succumbed to cancer. The cancer was discovered late, it had already metastasised. When the doctors told us about it, they were in effect giving us a prognosis that she had about three-months-or-so to live.

My grieving did not start after her death. It in fact started five months before her death. I had gone into grieving without knowing that I was already in what they term *anticipatory grief.*

Anticipatory Grief

If you had asked me about anticipatory grief before Tshidz's death I would have probably said that's just a thing psychologist created just to be seen as useful. In fact, the concept or thought of anticipatory grief had never crossed my mind. I knew absolutely Jack-squat about it.

But now I have a better understanding of it a lot more. Here is the thing about grief – though we think of it as something that happens *after* a death, it often begins long before death arrives. In my case with regard to Tshidz's death, grieving started as soon as we become aware that death is a likelihood. Once death is on the horizon, even just as a possibility, from my lived experience (I am not a psychologist) but I guess even from a psychological perspective it is natural that we begin to grieve.

Though this is different from the grief that follows a death, anticipatory grief can carry many of the symptoms of regular grief – sadness, anger, isolation, forgetfulness, and depression. I found this to be true in my case along my grieving journey. Indeed, these complicated emotions were often coupled with the exhaustion that came with being a caregiver (looking after Tshidz in her last days).

I was aware of the looming death and accepting it will come, which brought an overwhelming anxiety and dread. More than that, in advance of her death I grieved the loss of her abilities and independence, her loss of cognition, a loss of hope, loss of future dreams, loss of stability and security.

Reality is that this anticipatory grief is not just about accepting the future death, but of the many losses already occurring as an illness progresses.

When we know a death is imminent our bodies are often in a state of hyper-alertness – I panicked whenever she was unable to eat or was throwing up, I didn't know when or if an ambulance must be called. At times I felt completely helpless watching her lay in bed. It is a difficult time and situation when our loved one deteriorates. It was mentally and physically exhausting. The same is true of watching a loved one suffer, which is almost always part of a prolonged illness. Caring for Tshidz as she battled with cancer took an emotional toll on me. These things (and others) contributed to a sense of relief when the death eventually came, and a guilt that came with that relief.

I would like to think that these feelings are common and totally normal when someone has experienced an anticipated death. And yet we feel guilty for this relief, thinking it diminishes our love for the person. It doesn't, of course, but this relief can be a confusing feeling. We sometimes need to consciously remind ourselves that the relief does not change the deep love we had for the person, rather it is a natural reaction to the illness.

I went through all these emotions. I had to process it all and with time I learnt that when it comes to Grief – You can't go around it. You can't go over it. You can't go under it. You have to go THROUGH it or you have to go WITH it.

A part of me hoped she could fight and beat the cancer nonetheless, even the specialist who took care of her, pretty much wrote off any chances of her beating the cancer.

I lost hope when they told us there was no treatment that could be administered at that stage to fight or cure her cancer, but all they could do was manage her pain. She was effectively terminally ill.

It was a difficult time, what made it more difficult was that Tshidz chose not to announce or speak about her prognosis. In her words she said, "I do not want people to know that I have less than three months to live, I do not want people to mourn while I am still alive."

I had to respect that, but I was already grieving.

We had been together close to 20 years we had a 13-year-old son who was about to turn 14.

The three months that the doctors had given her became five months. And in that time, she managed to do a lot, including writing a book: *More Than A Woman; the power of inner peace.* Indeed she was more than a woman.

Never had I ever imagined what life would be without her, the words that are said when people get married, such as 'till death do us part' are such cliches that most of us never seriously consider their meaning or envision that reality of separation by death.

Her death caused me great sadness and grief; I never had anticipated that level of pain. I never thought I would miss someone so much.

When she died, I was so lost. I was totally blown apart my world temporarily froze; I was overwhelmed by grief. A part of me felt like giving up on life, but I could not, I could not be the cause of more grief for my son.

I had to pull myself together, I had a grieving son who had lost a mother.

His pain perhaps different to mine. I would like to think that my pain was not emanating from the same source as his. There are many different factors that affect how we grieve for a loved one, these include the relationship one had with the person who died, our previous experience of grief, and the support we have around us.

My take on this is that my pain came from an emotional connection that was born out of a friendship that grew into a loving relationship, she was my wife. Whereas my son's grief was born out of deeper stuff. Mothers connect differently to their children and that connection develops in the womb. It is not just emotional, it is a soul connection, a conception connection. A bond developed in the womb.

Research has suggested that, in some people, grief comes in stages or as a cycle. The grief cycle as a whole is often referred to as 'mourning' and describes how people adapt following a loss. It is a completely individual process but can be influenced by things such as culture, customs, rituals, and social expectations.

Having considered this, I realised that I had a duty, a responsibility, to care for our son. I chose life, and this meant that I had to figure out how to be a functional father and cope with grief.

Just when I thought things could not get any worse, serious family disputes erupted.

Some of Tshidz's very close family members (for reasons best known to them) accused me of killing her. They claimed that I had gone to Russia and acquired Polonium-210 and that I had poisoned her. This at the time was very disturbing and extremely distressing. It was so disheartening also that all her family, including her only brother and mother, chose to boycott her funeral.

With all that was going at the time, I withdrew myself and took up poetry and art as a way to comfort myself. But all this deepened my grieving and made me sadder. Surprisingly, most responses from those who engaged with my poetry and art thanked me for being honest about death and grief.

Close friends kept me going, I realised I needed to keep my hopes up. I am after all an ordinary person. I still have times when the same grief hits. I still wrestle with grief.

In the past three years I have understood myself better and made new friends. Some of them are fellow grievers, who have shared their stories with me. I realised that cultural differences and societal differences sometimes make people suffer grief alone. More-so those living in foreign lands (away from their native lands) it always seems like in times when one is grieving people walk away when they are most needed.

1

Grief Sucks

If I was a bird, I would just fly away.
If I was a bird, I would stretch my wings and soar above the clouds.
If I was a bird, I would tweet and sing my usual song.
But I am not a bird, I grieve, I cry, I am filled with emotion.
If I was a bird, I would fly to where you are. I love you; I miss you.
If I was a bird...

As I sat in the car after dropping my son at school, I looked up across the road at the end of that street and noticed there was a cemetery. I had never noticed it before. And suddenly, I was flooded with emotion. I thought of Tshidz and felt sorry for my son he now had to navigate life without his mother and so I typed the poem above on my phone.

It is often a common mistake that most of us make with regards grief when we generalise it and assume that grieving is the same process for everyone. Grief is not the same for everyone and it doesn't have a set expiry date and one never knows when bouts of unbridled emotions can just kick in or what triggers them. Never assume that because you cried at the funeral or mourned it is all done. Grief really sucks because it is a long process and often very unpleasant. It involves a range of emotions, feelings and actions which are likely to cause you pain and suffering. I learnt that these unpleasant phases and bouts of emotion are important parts of the grieving process and ignoring them or trying to disguise them in any way, may result in complicated grief. It is like I said important to allow the process, you must go THROUGH it, or you have to go WITH it.

Contrary to popular belief, grief is not the same for everyone and it doesn't have a set expiry date. Instead, it involves a range of emotions, feelings and actions which are likely to cause you pain and suffering. They are important parts of the grieving process and ignoring them or trying to disguise them in any way, is likely to result in complicated grief.

A number of clinicians and psychiatrists have come up with different grief models all of which aim to explain the grieving process and help the bereaved to "make sense of it". However, it is important to try and understand grief from different cultural standpoints simply because we don't grieve in the same way. Our cultural differences play an important role in the way we process and understand grieving.

Indeed, many people experience grief and a sense of loss after the death of a loved one. But the ways in which they experience and express these feelings may differ across cultures. Culture is the mix of beliefs, values, behaviours, traditions, and rituals that members of a cultural group share. Each culture has its own rituals that influence the expression of grief. Carrying out these practices offers a sense of stability and security. Rituals can also help people who are dying and bring comfort to the loved ones who are preparing for their loss.

Indeed, death evokes a variety of emotional responses, but the range of acceptable emotions and the extent to which the grief and sorrow experienced by mourners are allowed free expression are tied up with the unique institutions and values of each society.

The emotional tenor at funerals in England and other Western European societies tends, on the whole, to be rather low-key. While it is quite permissible for female relatives and other mourners to cry at funerals, the excessive display of grief in public is generally an embarrassment for both the bereaved and the comforter. In contrast, in some other cultures crying at funerals is not merely tolerated, it is required by custom, and at predetermined moments during the ceremony, the entire group of mourners may burst into loud and piercing cries.

In each culture, death is associated with rituals and customs to help people with the grieving process. Thus, rituals offer people ways to process and express their grief. They also provide ways for the community to support the bereaved. A person who is bereaved is in a period of grief and mourning after a loss. Death can create a sense of chaos and confusion. Rituals and customs provide a sense of routine and normalcy. They provide a set of directions that help structure the time surrounding death. Also, they direct people's roles during this time. Rituals and customs can help address a few scenarios such as how people care for people as they approach death. This includes who is present and what ceremonies are performed at the moments before and after death.

How a person's body is handled after death. This includes how the person's body is cleansed and dressed, who handles the body, and whether the body is buried or cremated. Whether grief is expressed quietly and privately or loudly and publicly. This includes whether public crying or wailing is appropriate. Whether people of different genders or ages grieve differently.

What rituals people perform after death and who is included in these rituals. How long family members are expected to grieve. And how they dress and behave during the mourning period.

How the deceased are honoured over the lifetime of the family. This includes ongoing rituals to celebrate or talk with the deceased. What new roles family members are expected to take on? This includes whether a widow remarries, or an oldest son becomes the family leader.

Traditionally in most cases Africans are brought up from childhood with a sense of belonging and relatedness with others. Individuals, thus, have a sense of obligation to a larger set of other individuals. This is one of the reasons why African tradition does not acknowledge the roles that advance care directives play in end-of-life decision-making for an incompetent patient. Instead, decision-making at the end-of-life period is left to the members of the family of the person concerned, an act which introduces unhealthy disagreement as events unfold.

Generally, Africans do not like facing the reality of death and often do not encourage the contemplation of death, be it their own death or the death of their loved ones. It is somewhat a taboo to think of or discuss one's death. Hence, people do not write their living wills or set aside money for their funeral while still alive, contrary to the practice in the western world. Death is also considered an enemy of life and Africans believe life should be preserved by all means even if the case is a hopeless one. The average African is not likely to discontinue life-sustaining treatment once it has commenced, and do not favour any artificial termination of life. Indeed, we cannot experience our world outside the cultural framework we bring to it. This implies that the distinction between grief as an internal, subjective process and mourning as its social expression is false.

The moment grief is expressed, it becomes mourning: death can only be experienced within a cultural context and grief can only be felt and expressed within cultural guidelines and expectations. Similarly, culture is such a crucial part of the context of bereavement that it's often impossible to separate an individual's grief from culturally required mourning. For example, in cultures with a belief system that says, 'do not grieve because the deceased has gone to a better life', it's difficult to assess accurately what seems to be muted grief: how do we distinguish where the cultural norm rules that demand muted grief end and 'real' grief begins?

Similarly, when the rules say 'cry', how do we tell whether the crying is genuine or merely conformity with cultural expectations? This suggests that the distinction between grief and mourning may be peculiar to Western culture.

Two other fundamental aspects of culture's influence on grief are its policing of grief; and its effect on how grief is handled.

The cultural dimension of death and grief has been studied by anthropologists for a long time: a community's rituals and beliefs facilitating the passage between life and death throw light on its beliefs and practices. For most of us, in our regular everyday activities, culture is 'invisible' precisely because it's all around us and is a major part of our assumptive world; it's as 'natural and unremarkable as the air we breathe or as the solid ground beneath our feet'.

Culture (from the Latin 'to cultivate') has a number of connotations, but in the context of bereavement and grief, culture has been used to refer to how a people or groups of people construe their world: culture provides the templates for how people represent their experience and is, therefore, the basis for their actions.

GRIEF AND GRIEVING
WHAT THE EXPERTS SAY

Dr Lois Tonkin presents an alternative to the grief models which are based on different phases, or stages, of grief. His theory teaches us that grief is constant and it stays the same but those affected by it grow around it. This model is also known as the "fried egg model of grief" – life is the big white circle and the yolk in the middle is the black hole left by the deceased person. The "egg yolk" is always there and forces us to grow our lives around it.

SIX R'S OF MOURNING

Dr Therese Rando has developed a model in which she takes the different emotional states a bereaved person is likely to go through and grouped them into three emotional categories – avoidance, confrontation, and accommodation.

The Six R's of Mourning are: **Recognise** the loss, **React** to the separation, **Recollect** and re-experience, **Relinquish** old attachments, **Re-adjust, Reinvest**.

RECONSTRUCTION OF MEANING

Robert A. Neimeyer sees grief as "a process of reconstructing a world of meaning which has been challenged by loss." This model is particularly well-suited to those struggling to get back to "pre-loss level of functioning." It employs constructivist therapy strategies in helping people to come to terms with their loss and find a way to move forward.

DUAL PROCESS MODEL OF GRIEF

Margaret Stroebe and Henk Schut's theory divides the grieving process into *loss-oriented* and *restoration-oriented* processes. The bereaved person oscillates between the two processes and in doing so, learns to balance the reality of their loss and learning to live life after it.

The Dual Process Model of Grief is suitable for men and those who struggle to confront their feelings and emotions. It encourages bereaved people to use restoration-oriented activities such as learning new skills and forming new relationships as a way of coping with grief and moving forward with life.

FOUR TASKS OF MOURNING

William Worden suggests that in order to complete their grieving process and move forward, the bereaved individual must accomplish four tasks:

Accept the reality of their loss, **process** their grief and pain, **adjust** to the world without their loved one in it, **find** a way to maintain a connection to their lost loved one whilst embarking on their own life

FIVE STAGES OF GRIEF

Although this is the most popular grief model, it was originally developed by Dr Elisabeth Kübler-Ross to explain the process terminally ill people go through after diagnosis: The Five Stages of Grief.

It's worth noting that grief is not as linear and predictable as this model suggests.

Different studies describe the stages of the grief cycle in slightly different ways, but the most common stages are:

Denial – feelings of shock, disbelief, panic or confusion are common here. "How could this happen?", "It can't be true".

Anger – blaming yourself, blaming others and hostility are all common feelings and behaviours – "Why me?", "This isn't fair", "I don't deserve this".

Depression – feeling tired, hopeless, helpless, like you have lost perspective, isolated or needing to be around others – "Everything is a struggle", "What's the point?".

Bargaining – feelings of guilt often accompany questions like "If only I had done more", "If I had only been…".

Acceptance – acceptance does not mean that somebody likes the situation or that it is right or fair, but rather it involves acknowledging the implications of the loss and the new circumstances and being prepared to move forward in a new direction.

These stages do not always appear in the same order for everybody, and some people experience some stages and not others. It is common to move forwards and backwards through the stages in your own way and at your own pace. Some people may experience grief outside of the cycle altogether.

2

Taking On The New Role; Single Parenting

My son had just turned 14 when his mother died. He had been aware of his mother's illness, but we had not divulged the details of her prognosis. He knew she had cancer and his hope was she would beat the cancer.

Indeed, most kids of his age and even younger know something about death. They've seen it on TV shows. But it's very different when it happens to someone close to them it is indeed a different reality when it is your mother.

I remember coming home from the hospital and breaking the devastating news to him, it was the most painful thing I have ever experienced. Watching his cry and expressing deep pain felt from the depth of his heart. As a parent I wished I could take away that pain, but I couldn't, I could not bring his mother back. Nonetheless, what I could do and still do is to help him cope in healthy ways.

The way teenagers respond to death is different from adults. They may sway from one mood to the next. That's normal. My son was lucky to have very supportive friends. He spent time with them at home and away from home; this was his way of coping with his feelings. It's also normal for kids to get angry, to feel sad, get anxious and to act younger or sometimes older than they are.

It's important to help your child express their feelings. I tried best I could to have him participate in the planning of his mother's funeral. I asked him for his input on several things and involved him and kept him informed.

I also found that it was helpful for me to express my own sadness because that in a way showed him that it's okay to be sad.

How your child behaves and how you respond depends on their age. Don't offer more information than they can understand.

My son had a very busy schedule he had just moved school and had after school activities. He enjoyed his street dance classes and something thing I learnt from that experience was keeping as much as possible of his normal schedule helped him feel secure.

After the death of a parent, it's normal for a child to worry about their surviving parent. It's helpful to reassure them you are okay and to communicate more and let them know if you are away from home. After the death of one parent, kids will worry about the other parent and need to be reassured that they're going to be around to take care of them.

My son found it a challenge to go to school at times my guess is going away from me at times made him anxious.

We worked through a lot of challenges and walked through the tough times hand in hand. The process of grieving is not easy. Adjusting to life without Tshidz was, and is, still difficult. Being a lone parent means that I have to be mother *and* father, and it is no walk in the park.

My son is a determined boy. He went on to do well in his GCSEs and he continues to do well. I am proud of who he has turned out to be despite the challenges of loss and grief that he has faced.

Whether or not to attend the funeral is a personal decision that depends entirely on you and your child. My son took a very active part with regards his mother's funeral. He was a pall-bearer and gave a very moving speech at his mother's funeral service.

Indeed, funerals can be an important part of the grieving process. They are a time to symbolically say goodbye and get on the path of accepting that a loved one is no longer here. When it comes to children attending funerals, there's no right or wrong thing to do. Instead, it's very context dependent. You need to ask yourself some questions: Is your child anxious, or easily distracted? Does he tend to dwell on things, or do they roll off his back? Is it going to be an open or closed casket? How long will the ceremony be? Does he even want to go? You should also consider how emotional people are going to be at the funeral. As a rule of thumb, it is wise not to expose your child to really scary, excessive displays of emotion. And when they are, we should explain that, even if the adults around them seem upset, they are still okay, safe, and will feel better again soon. Even more reassurance should be given if it is the child's primary caregiver who is very upset.

Funerals can be helpful for providing closure, but some children simply aren't ready for such an intense experience.

I was fortunate in this case because my son was able to deal with this ordeal. I would, however, advise never to force a child to attend a funeral. If your child wants to go, make sure that you prepare them for what they will see. Explain that funerals are very sad occasions, and some people will probably be crying. If there will be a casket you should prepare them for that, too.

I made sure that my son was comfortable with body viewing. I explained to him that the body might not look exactly like how his mother would have been. I was careful about this because her body had been in the mortuary for close to a month because of the family confusion and conflict with regards place of burial.

Another piece of advice that I would give is for you to keep in mind that even the best-prepared child might get upset, and that the child's behaviour can be unpredictable. Indeed, kids will not always behave in a way that you might want or expect. If you decide that a funeral is not the best way, there are other ways to have a goodbye.

In western influenced societies, there are other alternatives such as planting a tree, sharing stories, or releasing balloons; these can all be good alternatives for providing closure to a child.

Another thing I picked up from all this that I think is worth sharing is not to ignore your own grief, children will often imitate the grieving behaviour of their parents. It is important to show your emotions as it reassures children that feeling sad, or upset is okay. However, reacting explosively or uncontrollably teaches your child unhealthy ways of dealing with grief.

It can be particularly hard to help your child when you are also dealing with your own grief.

Many times, I worried that I was not 'doing it right' or that I was somehow making things worse.

Not having close family around or nearby made it very difficult for me. These are some of the challenges of being in the diaspora. You sometimes have to go through things alone. But remember that this is not something you have to do on your own. Your close friends become your family and I am eternally grateful for my friends, they filled in the gap.

I also put to good use the healthcare professionals and my child's school – they were very helpful.

My advice would be for you to take full advantage of the bereavement services that are local to you; they make the bereavement journey bearable. Make sure you have lots of support around you and other family members and friends who can support you.

Make sure also that you and your child are getting enough sleep, exercise, and healthy food. Looking after your physical health will help you all cope with your emotions too.

I am glad that my son and I go to the gym together and that we have made a commitment to eat healthy.

3

Family Conflicts: Bridges Burnt

A difficult time
Bridges burnt relationships, and previous ties undone, death reveals
much of that which in life was perfectly concealed.
They have said the worst of things – spoken of murder, abuse
and accused me of not loving and lack of affection.
From miles away they became experts
of day-to-day going's on in my household.
He was a Wife beater, abusive husband. He had divorced her,
he poisoned her, he never cared… and so they said.
But they neglect the critical questions:
Who was by her bedside in her last moments?
Who took her to all her doctor's appointments?
Who nursed her during the most difficult of times?
Most critically, with the professed knowledge of the so-called-abuse
and imagined divorce,
where were you in the critical time of need
when her days were numbered, and a prognosis given?
Time will vindicate, time will reveal, and time will heal.

Stories created history will know,
words said to assassinate and besmirch character will soon stick out
like a broken thumb, after all that's been said and done.
With bitter, twisted lies, they justified hate.
Found it worthwhile to attach and fix blame for a death caused by –
what medical experts pronounced as "naturally caused".
Cancer, Cancer, multiple organ failure, but not to them
Pongo killed her.
Trying to comfort and console each other in loss. They forgot
that we were all mourning. We were all hurting...
It's never easy to lose a loved one.
To you a daughter
To me a wife
To my son a mother.
But in grief you don't burn bridges,
you need not undo relationships...
but bridges you have burnt relationships you have unlocked and
vanquished, shredded and destroyed.
And so, we move on now without that link that once held us strong.
Posthumously they imagine divorce.
So, my in-laws trod me in the mud cry murderer, I withdraw
and allow if this is what comforts you.
Then have your cake and eat it.
My hands are clean, my conscience is clear, I have done my all
and now I move in the direction of the setting sun.
I wish you well.
But still, like dust, I'll rise to tell my side of the story.

Many families have experienced rifts or estrangements for a variety of reasons, both within immediate families and extended families. When a death occurs and the family is not intact, knowing how to reach out and deciding how to plan the funeral together is critically important; this can either help or worsen the grieving process depending on the path chosen. In some cases, a death can reconcile people who had been divided, and can reconnect those who were previously estranged or separated. In other cases, a death may do nothing to repair a falling-out. In my case it further aggravated a hostile situation and totally collapsed the relationship with my in-laws, particularly the ties between my mother-in-law and me.

There are many reasons that relationships are damaged or end, and sometimes those reasons seem meaningless considering a death, while at other times those reasons become magnified.

My personal experience with grief and the aftermath of Tshidz death, I learnt that any conflict between the living only robs the dead of their chance to be remembered. Even if you're in the right, the day of a funeral isn't about winning arguments, settling differences, or stirring up drama. I wanted to protect and preserve Tshidz's legacy and memory. She had lived a life of love and deserved a befitting funeral. However, the family squabbles after her death threatened to taint what was otherwise an admirable legacy and memory.

Tshidz's funeral was boycotted by her immediate family, for reasons best known to them. Weeks after her burial they held their own memorial service to which my son and I were not invited.

Undoubtedly, the vast majority of conflicts and squabbles in extended family relationships occur because of words miscommunicated, rumours told, lies spoken. Words are singularly the most powerful force available to humanity. We can choose to use this force constructively with words of encouragement, or destructively using words of despair. Words have energy and power with the ability to help, to heal, to hinder, to hurt, to harm, to humiliate and to humble.

We should weigh our words in every situation, especially during a time of bereavement. Those who speak out of anger or pain are usually reacting to people or situations and may say something hurtful that they later regret. Often, if you feel the tension rising among family members, words spoken in anger will only make things worse. It's important to stand up for yourself and express your opinion without attacking the position of others.

As we deal with family discord or difficult people, we need to be mindful of our emotions and what they are telling us. But more importantly, we need to ask, are my emotions a reflection of reality or a result of my potentially faulty conclusions? In other words, am I thinking clearly or through an emotionally blurred lens? It's important to answer these questions before taking the offensive against family members during an extremely emotional time.

I took care of my wife throughout her fight with cancer. She was at home and not in hospital for most of that period of illness, it was not easy in days that she was very sick. The only time I saw any of her relatives was after she died.

It was very hurtful for my in-laws to fabricate all the stories of divorce and poisoning when in truth they were not there in her time of sickness and on top of that they chose to boycott her funeral. No amount of truth twisting can fix that error. They tried to paint me the bad guy, they went on a social media campaign to besmirch my character, in efforts to justify their absence.

I do hope they all have found peace with themselves. I have forgiven, I hold no grudge, I found peace and I am moving forward.

Generally speaking, I have learned that what appears as greed and pettiness most times (generally) are really symptoms of survivors' struggle to feel loved and important. The fight for money and things – my daughter's or my son's belongings, – is not about the objects or the money itself, but about what they symbolise: importance, love, security, self-esteem, connectedness, and immortality.

The old adage that "money makes people do funny things" doesn't do justice to the real problems and root causes of family conflict. Money is not the core reason that families fight; money is how we keep score in the fight for the intangibles of love, approval, and primordial survival. Money and possessions also help allay the fears of those left behind. When families fight, greed is rarely the principal motive.

The genesis of the issues of those who usually fight for the deceased's possessions can almost always be traced back several years, if not all the way back to childhood. For some, the trouble starts with the involvement of nonfamily: "everything changed when he or she married," or "She was providing for all my needs until she married him, and he started calling the shots." It is clear that inheritance conflict doesn't come out of the blue; it is a continuation of long-term relationship problems that resurface upon the illness or death of a loved one. And they aren't just about money or greed; they are about more, much more. But what is it that so often drives people to wage war against their own flesh and blood over a loved one's estate?

There are five basic reasons why families fight in matters of inheritance: First, humans are genetically predisposed to competition and conflict; second, our psychological sense of self is intertwined with the approval that an inheritance represents, especially when the decedent is a parent; third, we are genetically hardwired to be on the lookout for exclusion, sometimes finding it when it doesn't exist; fourth, families fight because the death of a loved one activates the death anxieties of those left behind; and finally, in some cases, one or more members of a family has a partial or full-blown personality disorder that causes them to distort and escalate natural family rivalries into personal and legal battles. These sources of family conflict are not mutually exclusive; in most cases, some combination of the five elements present themselves in a combustible cocktail of family rivalry and conflict. I experienced some of the worst but best advice I would give having been there is let those who want material possessions have them. Your peace is more valuable than kitchen utensils and money.

4

Merging Western Cultures with African Traditions

African death rituals evolved when the traditional religious beliefs of Africa were challenged and modified by the spread of Christianity and Islam on the continent.

Hence, it is a confusing and difficult thing to balance cultural practices and follow certain African traditions to fulfil the requirements of a safe passage after death more-so for those in the diaspora.

Funerals conducted in the diaspora for those relocated in foreign countries have become sites of contestation and confusion, as culture, spirituality and adopted foreign cultures collide. Many people remain befuddled as to how to balance new-found mixture of foreign customs with their African cultures. Balancing the standard Christian or Islamic ways and the observance or completion of culturally appropriate African rituals.

Every culture since civilisation tends to the appropriate care of its dead and most of them have three things in common as far as disposition of the dead matters. Firstly, the organisation of some type of funeral rites, rituals, and ceremonies. Secondly, the securing of a sacred place for burying the dead and thirdly, memorialising of the dead.

It is all joy anytime a child is born; however, death presents a direct contrast. Even when people die at ripe old ages, they are mourned by their families extensively or briefly depending on the culture in which the death occurs.

There are cultural and social variation in the way funerals are conducted for Zimbabweans in the diaspora depending on tribal cultural beliefs, family traditions and religious affiliation (most Zimbabweans are of Christian persuasion).

That said, it is worth noting that even back in Zimbabwe there are also differences between urban and rural areas. In urban areas, people are generally buried in cemeteries and much of the commemoration takes place in church. In the villages all the rituals related to funeral practice, including the burial, happen at the homestead of the bereaved family.

The first consideration is for the body to be bought home, physically and spiritually. For those who die in urban areas, a process of 'fetching the spirit' occurs before the deceased is transported back to the rural home (village). Relatives in the city ensure that the body is first taken from the hospital, or morgue, back to the urban place of residence to make peace with those who are living there, before embarking on the longer journey.

In the rural village, news of the death is made public and shared with the headman, who will help the family choose an appropriate funeral date. It is considered undesirable to have more than one burial per day. Rural funerals are large affairs, which attract crowds of several hundred people, including kin, neighbours, and urban visitors.

In the week before the funeral weekend, young women from the village help the family prepare the homestead and the food for the guests while young men help dig the grave. After the body arrives from the city or is fetched from the local mortuary, the body is then washed and the ritual, (washing of the body) is performed while the elders and family members deliver messages to the deceased to prepare them for safe passage to the afterlife. The body is dressed in 'new clothes' in preparation for display during the funeral rites. This often takes place at the local mortuary, where the body is dressed by selected family members. If the person is a church member, they will be dressed in their church uniform.

However, all these rituals cannot be performed in most of the cases in the diaspora because the funeral directors do most if not all the preparations following the regulations and customs of the local authorities. This is what happened in Tshidz's case, I remember her mother had instructed some of her friends to dress her body and do certain things. But I had to tell them that the dressing of the corpse was going to be done by the funeral directors at the funeral parlour, therefore they needed not to worry.

Indeed, there are cultural differences between our adopted western ways of conducting funerals and how things are done in Zimbabwe.

For example, in Zimbabwe the night before the funeral, the body would be placed in the main house where members of the immediate family and close friends communicate with the deceased and prepare the spirit for its passage, also recalling their life and achievements in private. Religious leaders may join the vigil.

The funeral starts early the next morning as the body is moved to a tent in the yard where a larger gathering assembles. The coffin is normally closed to avoid exposing the deceased to a wider public, some of whom might harbour feelings of jealousy and envy, wanting to bewitch the body. This is why trusted close friends and family share their last thoughts and respects in the house, before the wider public arrive.

A funeral programme might include as many as a dozen speakers, including family, friends, neighbours, colleagues, religious leaders and a speaker from the house of the traditional leader. The latter needs to affirm that the deceased caused no ill or harm to the community during life. This part may last several hours, before the religious leaders walk with the coffin to the grave site as they speak of the life after death. As the body is lowered into the grave, handfuls of soil are tossed into the grave, a practice known to symbolise the passage from dust to dust.

In truth some of these practices are incorporated even in the western cultures, we tossed handfuls of soil into Tshidz's grave. Like death rituals in many other cultures, African death rituals are steeped in its traditions, cultural beliefs and religions indigenous to the continent for centuries. Though religious and modern influences bring change to traditional death customs, many of the elements of the past survive in Africa and in the death rituals of people of African descent in the new world.

It is common practice among many Zimbabweans not to keep their dead in the morgue for a long time. It is never more than two or three days in most cases.

Mourning goes on for as long as it takes to prepare and plan the burial and continues even after the deceased has been buried. In Zimbabwe, the adopted 'traditional' dress colour for mourning the dead is black or the church uniform of those who wear uniforms to church.

In more recent cases, the dress code for funerals has evolved with people opting for other colour themes. It has become usual, for organisers of such funerals to incorporate and merge western culture with African traditions at funerals as their desire to celebrate the passing of the dead rather than mourn them. This happens to be the case sometimes when the deceased lived longer or might have died younger but made tremendous achievements in their lives that impacted many people or for other reasons.

Tshidz's funeral was one such and yellow was the colour chosen by my son to honour her with.

In decades past, Zimbabwean funerals have been organised in much simpler ways to cut down on cost, however, this is no longer the case in these modern days. In recent times funerals among Zimbabweans and Africans in the diaspora and back home in their respective home countries, funerals for Africans have almost become a show of not only flamboyance but creativity. In some cases, funerals are now major displays of extravagance in most parts of Zimbabwe and Africa in general. Families try to outdo each other in terms of who organised the best and most expensive funeral(s). In certain parts of Zimbabwe, funerals are major platforms where people go to display their affluence.

As previously said, a unique feature about funerals among Zimbabweans today is that they have become flamboyant, so much so that some sections of society are getting troubled about it as some Zimbabweans in and out of the country would have preferred that the deceased is buried solemnly and gracefully in an inexpensive manner, simply because the dictates of today's glamorous funerals among Zimbabweans impose huge expenses.

The pressures to organise elaborate and showy funerals have compelled many people who do not have the money for such to go ahead and do it all the same. Most often than not, this becomes detrimental to a grieving family as they are saddled with debt problems afterwards. People continue to indulge in such funeral extravagance, and it appears not to be solely a Zimbabwean thing as cultures across Africa and the globe are guilty of this phenomenon.

Questions need to be asked as to the efficacy of the emerging culture that is signalling an end to the sombre funeral. Mourners are increasingly arriving in bright colours or fancy dress for celebratory ceremonies.

People are turning away from churches and tears for family funerals in favour of celebrations at home, in the park, on the beach – or even the office.

One in two funeral directors say that they have been asked to arrange a 'destination funeral' rather than a church or crematorium.

Just as marriages have moved away from religious buildings and register offices, now people want to take funerals to new locations, introducing fun and even fancy dress to the occasion.

It seems like even the dead have to keep up with the Joneses, with bespoke funerals all the rage. Themed, bespoke funerals are becoming more popular. We are seeing a culture shift in the way that we deal with loss. It's becoming ever more common to hear people refer to funerals as a celebration of life.

Indeed, there is no harm in doing this for families that can afford such funerals, nonetheless spare a thought for those pressured to do this and end up impoverished.

Perhaps serious and constructive discussions need to be held with regards the culture of feasting at funerals particularly in some African countries *(dignified send offs or burials should not be benchmarked by the amount of food available at the funeral)* that mindset must be challenged.

The 'cultural' practice of feasting at funerals needs to be

denounced, I would argue that it is a form of corruption that impoverishes the bereaved families in some cases. Imagine a poor widow's son who is forced to slaughter the only milk cow he owns in order to prepare a decent meal for the mourners. It is time we openly challenge some of these practices that we have conveniently labelled 'cultural' or 'traditional'.

5

Where to bury?

There are some very pragmatic reasons that we should be concerned about with regards where people are buried.

Millions of people die every year in the world, each leaving behind a variable number of close attachments, especially for those closest to the deceased, an intensely emotional and disruptive period often follows the loss, gradually attenuating as the reality of the death is comprehended and accepted and its consequences appreciated.

The experience of a loved one's death is highly stressful, both because of the loss and also because of confrontation with mortality. Additionally, a myriad of stressors emerge as a consequence of requirements to attend to a range of things not usually on the agenda. Coping with these is necessary for restoration of ongoing life.

A deceased loved one thus bequeaths an array of emotional and practical problems that a bereaved person must solve. Given the scope and magnitude of the impact of losing a loved one, it is notable that relatively few negative long-term consequences usually occur.

Some people meet the coping demands, with the help of supportive friends and family, and find a pathway that leads to restoration of a potentially satisfying and meaningful life. However, a significant section of bereaved people, does not cope effectively with bereavement. Instead, they become entangled in grief, caught up in a futile struggle of silent protest, trying to avoid reminders, and being carried helplessly on endless waves of acutely painful emotion. This could also lead to displaced anger, a reactionary defence mechanism and a maladaptive coping strategy.

My mother-in-law might have, in my view, used the issue of 'place of burial' as an outlet for her anger, (displaced anger). There are times in the natural grieving process for the individual to feel frustrated, trapped, and hurt. It is common to have those churning emotions surface and be directed toward someone or something. When pain dominates the feelings, it is natural to look for someone to blame. Being angry is a way of releasing energy, of protesting a loss that does not make sense or seem fair. Even though deep down one understands that anger is not logical or justified, emotions are rarely logical.

Tshidz and I had moved to England, and we had naturalised our stay, becoming British citizens. I still consider myself Zimbabwean, however legal documents that we both held recognise us as British.

So, when Tshidz passed on the question arose as to where she would be buried?

Her mother wanted her body repatriated to Zimbabwe for burial. Initially I had agreed nevertheless after consultation and much consideration I opted to honour Tshidz's wish which was to be buried in England.

Tshidz and I, had, had these conversations before and she had expressed her wish to be buried in England. When I voiced this to her family it was not well received.

This became a point of conflict and could have been part of the reason why her family (mother, brother and cousins boycotted the funeral).

It was a difficult time a decision had to be made. I had considered the pros and cons of burying her in Zimbabwe, how this would have impacted on my son. I wanted my son to be able to visit his mother's grave. I considered what was best for my son and most of all I wanted her wishes honoured.

There are some things that culture demands that are not fit for purpose in our day and age. Practices that allow family elders to override decisions that the deceased would have made. I was not willing to allow that to happen and thus, I stood my ground much to my in-law's chagrin.

Anger is born out of misunderstanding

Everyone wants to be understood. It's a common human desire, and a gift we can give one another. How do we give this gift? Truly listening, asking what someone would like rather than thinking we know what they need, and communicating our own needs clearly to those we love are a few of the ways to begin to understand and to be understood. Also, it is sometimes helpful to gain knowledge of the cause of some of the behaviours that create stress. It is much easier to respond to angry, contrary behaviour if we know what some of the causes are.

Anger is the cause of the most troubling behaviour – either our own or others'. Sometimes angry responses are a mystery to us: Where did that come from? What did I do to deserve that response? It helps to know that the root of most angry behaviour is hurt or fear. If we get to the cause of the anger and admit it (being hurt or afraid), we have a chance to understand ourselves, to deal directly with the root cause, and make an apology if we want to.

Indeed, funerals can be an important part of the mourning process for surviving family and friends. They are a time to celebrate the person's life, share memories and provide and receive support. Each culture, religion and spiritual group have their own specific funeral rites and practices that prescribe how to remember or honour the deceased, as well as to help those left behind to cope with the grieving process. These rituals can be vastly different across groups.

And having married in a different tribe this boiled down to a tribal conflict as tensions arose because of my decision to bury Tshidz in England.

Some shit-stirrers tried to make a mountain out of this ant-hill by taking this family standoff to social media, the hope perhaps was to solicit tribal support or put pressure on me to backdown. (It became a Shona versus Ndebele thing) social media threads on why people should not marry across tribes were started mostly by people who did not even understand the relationship dynamics that held Tshidz and I together. I ignored most of the nonsense that some shameful people spewed under the so-called Mtwakazi banner. But I digress.

Admittedly it would have allowed for more relatives and close family friends to attend her burial had we buried her in Zimbabwe.

But it was not about costs or numbers, it was a matter of principle. In addition to that the logistics involved would have been a nightmare.

I was already up to my neck with stress from the loss. The grief had also brought with it additional pressure. The outcome of this standoff was a manifestation of anger, from my in-laws as opposed to understanding.

Anger during grief can often be displaced and/or expressed in puzzling ways to others around us. We may be angry with the loved one who died and left us behind, we might be angry with God for taking our loved one from us, we could be angry with the disease that brought about the death. It may be easier to express anger to someone nearby than to try to figure out just whom or what we are really angry with; so, the ones who get the blast of our anger are usually our nearest and dearest – those we would not want to hurt at all.

Some of the unspoken difficulties of coming from an African culture and living in a Western society when grieving or mourning is that this blend of cultures tells you how you should grieve. It's insidious and subtle, but the instructions and latent expectations are there. Grieve quietly and in private. Expect people to feel sorry for you and feel comforted in their sympathy. Know that people will only care up until the funeral or memorial service; then they'll continue on with their own lives. Be gracious with people's verbal fumblings, the empty phrases, and the Hallmark cards and flowers offered up.

There isn't room for anything other than sadness. Especially not anger. But those who are bereaved, as I learned, can be really angry. Because I lacked the support and understanding I needed as I grieved and grieved mostly alone.

Anger felt during grieving is one thing that is often overlooked a lot of times those comforting you assume it is just sadness.

But as I went through the grieving process, I felt a lot of anger and frustration. At first, I didn't even recognise these feelings for what they were. These feelings are not comfortable feeling, let alone expressing them to those around me.

My anger manifested in an abject form of isolation. I pushed a lot of people away. I cut others off. I wasn't vaguely interested in making any new friends. Most of it felt warranted at the time. Other parts were grief and sadness with nowhere else to go. My rage helped me to feel connected to my wife. If I wasn't seething about the sucky hand I had been dealt, who was I? And if I did disconnect from it, would it mean disconnecting from Tshidz and forgetting her? The fear of that kept me locked into being mad and perpetually ruminating on all the ways I had been wronged.

It was stumbling upon a tweet that finally caused something to break and shift. The tweet was from psychotherapist and grief counsellor Megan Devine and contained a graphic with words from her book *It's OK That You're Not OK*. They read:

> The reality of anger never gets any airtime in our culture.
> Anger is a response to a sense of injustice. Of course, you're angry; whatever has happened to you is unjust.
> Anger, allowed expression, is simply energy.
> Shown respect and given room, anger tells a story of love and connection and longing for what is lost.
> Contrary to pop psychology and the medical model, anger is healthy, normal, and necessary.

"Your anger surrounding your loss is welcome," Devine wrote in the tweet. *"It's healthy. It's not something to rush through so you can be more 'evolved' or acceptable to the people around you."*

I remember feeling a sense of being understood when I read those words. But I also felt this levity that I could accept my anger as a by-product of loss. I had every right to be angry about losing Tshidz and all the things I had lost as a result of her death. What human wouldn't be mad about having to scramble to feel some sort of normalcy when their sense of grounded-ness is taken from underneath them so tragically?

My anger was OK. How I had been coping with grief was the best way I knew how.

6

All kitchen utensils belong to the woman; when cultural practices are used vindictively

Death brings out the best and worst in families. Cultural traditions can be abused and weaponised and used to hurt others.

Indeed, the death of a loved one can have a major impact on family unity.

At a time of grieving the loss of a loved one each individual family member must reconcile the end of their physical relationship with the person who died and their ongoing grief over the loss. Unfortunately, this often means that at a time when the family could benefit from being closer than ever, misunderstandings and differences set them at a distance.

My journey through grief saw me at loggerheads with my in-laws over what in hindsight appears very petty.

Personally, I don't express my love through gifts, objects, or money. My values have never been grounded in materialism in any way. Thus, I yielded all and did not claim any of my wife's possessions even that which we shared in our 18 years of marriage. Yet all of a sudden, my in-laws were scrambling for stuff – much of it being stuff they hadn't cared about or wanted until after my wife's death.

As hard as it is for many of us to admit, some family members become wide-eyed and want to know what material possessions have been left behind by the deceased, and what they can get, even those who we had never imagined could get entangled in conflict over material things all of a sudden get involved in the issues of estates and belongings.

Some people are opportunistic and greedy. I won't try and deny this reality. I've seen it on my journey with grief.

Previously in my work as a journalist I had come across some horror stories of family greed and, frankly, some of them were so unbelievable however, what I went through will threaten to destroy your faith in humanity.

I'm concise of the fact that not all in-laws are bad there are a lot more families out there that unite and work together in things of grieving.

There are also quite a few scenarios in which people's actions have been labelled as selfish when, in reality, the motives behind them were far more complex than assumed.

In truth, grief can make us all a little egocentric and it can be difficult to empathise with another person's feelings, actions, and grief reactions. In my experience I picked out two common reasons for such behaviour – anxiety and uncertainty –

These can increase a person's tendency to assume that others see things exactly as they do. On top of this, our human brains are even more predisposed to making assumptions about people who we are close with and who we perceive as similar to us – like family members – perhaps because we assume these people share the same values, attitudes, and worldview.

Nonetheless that's not always the case. I thought that my inlaws where Christians and as Christians they would lean more towards the western attitudes and culture with regards how we would conduct ourselves during and after the funeral.

But I found out that they would pick and choose from the African culture and western culture depending on what was convenient for them to achieve their desired end.

My son and I were left with not a single kitchen utensil. This is just a trivial matter because we were able to go to the supermarket to get new utensils.

My bone to chew with regards this is how at times families take advantage of and abuse cultural practices.

No consideration was given with regards what was taken from the house (kitchen).

I personally had no issues getting new stuff nonetheless the same could not be said about my son.

People grieve at their own pace. One family member might feel ready to go through a loved one's belongings, while another can't stand the thought of it. Neither is right or wrong, they may just be grieving at different paces.

My thoughts are that great care has to be taken to avoid stressing a child who is already mourning.

It was a confusing time for my son. His grandma and aunties had boycotted the funeral. His only uncle had also stayed away. It was a delicate situation for me to try to balance. I never want to disconnect my son from his grandmother, she is the only grandparent that my son has.

I had hoped that she would at least be there for my son and for her daughter but her dislike for me was stronger than I thought. Indeed, death brings out the best and worst in families.

My mother-in-law came to England soon after Tshidz died but she did not come to our house. She only came to collect Tshidz's clothes and came in when my son was in school.

What was sad is that my son only got to meet his grandmother two months after his mother's death.

It was on his mother's birthday. We decided to go to the cemetery to place flowers on Tshidz's grave. As we were walking back to the car his grandmother and his aunt, and a few other relatives happened to be walking into the cemetery. A strange and rather awkward place for my son to meet his grandmother.

Nonetheless, my son was delighted to see his grandmother but also very emotional about that brief encounter. The meeting was really brief he basically just went up to her gave her a hug and exchanged greetings and followed me to the car.

The situation was very awkward, my son had questions. 'When did 'gogo' arrive?' Why hasn't she come to stay with us? Where is she staying?"

These were questions that I carefully tried to answer on our drive back home.

I had no idea of the exact date that she arrived in England, to this day I don't know.

I knew she had been around soon after Tshidz was buried.

Her primary interest seemed to have been focused on getting Tshidz's belongings her grandson was secondary. I don't doubt or question her love for her grandson, she must love him, he is after all her only grandson from her only daughter.

I know we all grieve differently and like I have already said grief can at times cause us to behave in very strange ways.

I assumed that whatever anger that she had over her daughter's death, she found a way to channel that towards me. I became the object upon which she unleashed that anger. I had no issues with that, but I took issue with attempts to use my son as a tool to get at me.

A lot of falsehoods and creatively crafted stories were said and messaged to my son. Very hurtful things that disturbed him a lot.

Imagine your grandmother telling you that your father caused the death of your mother, he poisoned her. It was unacceptable and verging on abuse and criminal. But I stayed calm I tried not to respond or retaliate. I kept my peace.

I reached out to my brother in-law Tshidz's brother based in Canada and requested that he speaks to his mother and ask her to stop sending these text messages to my son.

His response was 'show me the messages, why do you hate my mother so much? Now you are trying to get her arrested in England.' I couldn't believe it and so I let it go.

But I knew it would stop, and I was glad it did. I was the one living with a grieving child whose mental state was broken by grief and all these added stresses caused by the shenanigans of my in-laws was not in the least bit helpful.

Understandably, people have different grieving styles. Although people typically think of emotions when they think about grief, some people grieve in a much more hands-on way. I would say, I became an instrumental griever.

What made me feel better was when I took action or did something in my grief. I looked after my son physically and emotionally and took great care of protecting Tshidz's legacy and her reputation. I did not care for personal belongings. I refrained from all the public displays of family confrontations that the in-laws tried to draw me into.

At one point I got a call from a journalist who runs a tabloid type online publication. He had my mother-in-law on the call wanting to discuss private family grief on this live broadcast. I declined and respectfully ask the journalist to respect my privacy in my time of grieving.

When I enquired as to why my mother in-law was having to take the route of engaging the media, instead of consulting members of my family to help resolve whatever issues that she thought could be sorted by going live on some broadcast.

I realised that this was an attempt to soil my name, and an attempt for her to play victim. I gathered that all her shenanigans were aimed at not only distracting attention from herself guilt for not being present during her daughter's illness and boycotting her daughter's funeral.

Sad as it was it did not anger me. Nonetheless it upset me. I concluded that she has a strange way of grieving.

On her second visit to our house, she came to collect the kitchen utensils. She came early in the morning, and it was then that my son got to see his grandmother. For the first in our home.

He woke up to the sounds and cutlery being packed away in boxes and I remember he sat by the stairs watching all the drama unfold.

They took the cookie jar with cookies in it and all other containers with the contents in them, the rice container, sugar, salt I mean all. I knew this had nothing to do with cultural practices but just a vindictive act.

My mother in-law's friend who had driven her to our house even tried to talk her out of some of this pleading "but there is a child what will he use what will he remember her with?" But this plea fell on deaf ears.

The friend then asked my son to pick a few items to keep, he took two items a coffee mug and a tray. Indeed, some objects become special and significant after a loved one's death.

After all was packed and loaded in her friend's car, she spoke with my son for a bit and as they walked to the car to drive off, she took a few photos with him and that was it she left.

7

Culture and new times

For most culturally inclined Zimbabwean men and women, grieving a lost spouse is a process that includes traditional funeral rites, ceremonies to ensure spiritual health and community support, but it can also include suspicion and questions around the circumstances of the spouse's death. Most of the people across the tribal divide in the country normally visit traditional healers or consult spiritualists to ascertain the cause of death, never minding any post-mortem report from medical professionals.

These purported cultural practices exacerbate the often complex and multifaceted grieving process.

There is a strong held believe that persists in many tribal cultures that there is always a person who has caused the death and there must always be a 'witch' to blame for any death.

In some instances, some tribes discourage the bereaved or the grieving from crying, the argument being it will lead others to cry. But l would encourage people to cry, to actually deal with grief.

There is, however, a difference in how widows are treated as opposed to the way widowers are treated.

In some cases, and some tribes in Zimbabwe traditional healers, tell widows that culturally, there are rituals that must be done to separate the living spouse from the spirit of their deceased partner.

Widows are instructed to throw their undergarment in the

grave of their husband, a practice to ensure that the spirit of the husband will not continue to be with her. There are other requirements too.

One must wait for a period of one year before they engage in any sexual relationship with someone else, and they can only do so after a cleansing ceremony.

After a year, there is a cleansing ceremony, where women are required to jump a "knobkerrie", a short stick with a rounded top, to show that she has not engaged in any sexual relationship during that period. If she fails to jump, it will show that she would have done so. These are some cultural practices that some view as not consistent with the modern times.

There is an ongoing and broader debate as to the spiritual benefits or lack thereof in the cultural practices that once were the dominant way of life in Africa before colonialism swept most of these traditions away.

Colonialism across most of Africa was so thorough – especially among the former British protectorates – that in its aftermath Africa was essentially hollowed out. The civilisations of the people, their various cultures and traditions, their religions, political philosophies, and institutions, were eroded or even destroyed.

Today most of our African cultures should not even be called African cultures, but Afro-Christian infused cultures. The language, political ideology, socio-economic structures, education, and everything that makes informs our traditional cultures, now has a touch of western or Christian influence.

Even that which we refer to as popular culture, does not originate from within our countries. African nations now have a total dependency on foreign political philosophies and ideas, and their shifts and movements. Thus, even that which we currently refer to as African funeral will have a priest reading a Bible as part of burial rites.

It is the feeblest position a state and its people can be in because it is a position of chronic subservience. It also means that whatever becomes normalised in the west will eventually be adopted in, say, the most rural part of Zimbabwe.

This has resulted in all our traditional cultures drying out and Africa being slowly emptied of its essence, and becoming a relic, no different in substance from a statue or a museum.

Increasingly, our leaders and the prominent amongst us as Africans have joined up in tell us that the way of the west is "modern" and "civilised", echoing the early colonialists who dismissed our civilisations as "barbaric", "archaic", and "uncivilised" to install theirs. They tell us that our institutions are corrupt, that our societies are patriarchal, and that the African traditional religions are heathenish. As western supremacy entrenches itself in our psyche, we are developing a complex that embraces western ideas without considering whether they are compatible with our own political, social, economic, and cultural system.

Losing a spouse is a painful experience for widows across Zimbabwe. Tribes living within Zimbabwe often share a local culture rich with rituals and extended family support meant to help the widow deal with the loss. The open culture of discussing grief in churches and with neighbours is also important to the healing process.

Zimbabwean funerals are a community affair in which the whole community feels the grief of the bereaved and shares in it.

The purpose of the activities preceding the funeral is to comfort, encourage and heal those who are hurting.

Some of these cultural funeral practices are still practiced by Zimbabweans in the diaspora nonetheless parts of these practices are now diluted with a touch of western culture and other bits and bobs from other parts of Africa.

In the Shona culture, the largest indigenous group in Zimbabwe, spouses are expected to give an account of what caused the death.

I remember having to give the account of what had happened to Tshidz over and over, I was not really required to, but I guess those who came to condole with me felt it cultural to ask (What happened) and as such I had to give the obligatory response and narrate the events.

Alternatively, Zimbabweans and all Africans living in the diaspora might have to rethink the question: where is home? We must see the world as a common home that should be shared by all and for their well-being. Maybe home could be redefined, not only in terms of where one was born but also in terms of where one lives with one's immediate family.

Indeed, the experience I went through after my wife's death got me thinking, other than the cultural reasons given by family members back in our countries of origin those of us in the diaspora need to ask ourselves a bold question: What is wrong with being buried in a foreign land? After all, what is a foreign land, given the fact that many Zimbabweans have found a home on British soil and have established families in England? Some Zimbabweans have married women or men on these shores.

Others have established businesses that have created jobs for both foreigners and locals.

Therefore, it can be reiterated, where is home for such individuals?

8

Grieving and social media

Tshidz was a social media fanatic she would post and document a whole lot, from motivational stuff, inspirational and empowerment to personal reflections of her day-to-day life. She was an avid user of Facebook and Instagram.

Her last post on Facebook was a post about our son. It was simple but deep in meaning. She posted a picture of our son with the caption:

"My joy, My hope. My everything. My strength".

It was as if she knew this would be the last thing she would post. Those words have strengthened and motivated our son in many ways, and I know he cherishes that post. Indeed, he was her joy.

I cannot begin to imagine what she was going through her mind as she laid in that hospital bed hours before she died.

Earlier that day she had asked me to bring our son to visit her in hospital. She asked me to leave the room and I left her in there with our son and they talked for a while.

In her last days she made sure we took photos almost every day. My son and I would complain almost always as she would take these selfies with us for her social media content.

Nonetheless, today we see the method in that madness as we now realise, she left a capsule of memories we hold dear and enjoy today.

One interesting thing that social media has given us is documentation of our lives, in our own words. Looking through Tshidz's social media profiles we see a documentation of her life and memories. Her social media platforms are full of her thoughts, blog posts, pictures, things she found enjoyable or interesting. It's almost like an open diary that she left behind for her loved ones to look through it and hear her voice again.

Indeed, it was difficult and emotional to scroll through her social media accounts when the grief was still fresh. However, over time, though, these moments, posts, videos, and pictures have become cherished ways to bring her voice and memory back to us.

While the grieving process isn't new, social media has only become an intricate part of everyday life in the last decade or so. This newer communication method has become a fairly integral part of the grieving process for many, because so much of our day-to-day lives is shared and documented through social media networks.

The rapid growth of social media over the past number of years has been built on our desire to post we post pictures from last night's pub crawl; The church service pictures, updated images of your cousin's new baby; vacation highlights. It seems like these platforms were built for just this – a sharing tool that allows us to show our friends and family how very exciting/enviable/amazing our lives are.

But then, ironically, death gets in the way. To be alive is to know that death is always lurking around the corner – or in today's world, waiting to be revealed via our social media newsfeed.

Yes, hashtags have come to be the modern-day harbinger of death, the grim reaper's tool of choice. Inevitably as life goes, we are getting more accustomed seeing sad hashtags filling our feeds, ones that start with the dreaded #RIP.

As with anything, there are some positive and negative aspects involved in social media sharing. Mainly because grief is such a heightened and powerful emotion, both the positive and negative aspects can be received in an intensified way.

I remember how my son would get so upset at some of the things that were shared after his mother's death in the comment section on his mother's page.

Some of Tshidz's school friends from (Usher Institute) had taken it upon themselves to explain what they thought had happened to her. They spread a lot of misinformation and hurtful things.

Understandable, my son responded nastily to some of them but in time I told him to ignore most of these gossipers and merchants of falsehoods and confusion.

For those grieving, indeed, social media can give you a platform to speak from. It allows you to connect with other people you know and even strangers across the world. The connections you make through social media can be exceptionally close, even if you're not seeing each other in person.

For many people, social media offers a support system of friends to talk to, interact with, and share intellectual musings.

I, for one shared part of my grieving through poetry which I posted on social media. I have a strong network on social media, this became an excellent outlet to allow me to talk about my grief, honour my wife, and have supportive friends to console me. All of this can be a healthy way to process grief.

Veritably, social media gives you a way to honour friends and relatives who have passed on. Creating a post with pictures and loving words offers a creative outlet for your thoughts. It gives you an audience who can read about your loved one and share in your memories. It allows mutual friends to share their own grief, building a loving way to remember the person who passed and support each other.

I remember that it was through social media that I announced Tshidz death to most of my friends, of course I took the precaution and curtesy to call family and closest friends to inform them through the traditional way.

Social media also allows you to share news, such as the dates of memorial services and any types of honorary events or charity drives that involve the person who passed. Overall, these aspects of social media allow you to process your grief in a positive and supportive way.

Not everyone was happy with the way I used social media to announce Tshidz death I remember her cousin (sister) from Wolverhampton telling me to remove the post. I did not buy her logic or argument about the post. I understand that there are some who are old school out there and prefer to do things the traditional way, but then again why would they take offence if they can see the post, it means that they are on Facebook, so I really didn't get the farce. I know I can be hard-headed, but I stand my ground when I think I am right and, in this case, I think I was.

Here is some etiquette with regards posting about a death.

Please pause and consider your role and relationship to the newly deceased. Know your place. My advice to those distant to the deceased would be when you hear of someone's death before you post anything to social media wait and then wait a little longer before posting anything. Again, I say know your place. This may seem trivial, silly, and not worth talking about, but I promise you it isn't.

If the person is married, let the spouse post first.

If the person is "young" and single, let the partner, parents, or siblings post first.

If the person is "old" and single, let the children post first.

If you can't identify the family/inner circle of the person, you probably shouldn't be posting at all.

Understandably, social media is often mentioned with negative connotations. Most of the downside of social media has very little to do with the technology but, the way it's being used or abused rather.

Some people use social media in a less than healthy way where grief is concerned. They are fraudulently raising money. This can have a negative impact for those who are truly grieving because it is hurtful to see people fraudulently use the death of a loved one in that way.

Many random and indeed some popular Zimbabwean women's Facebook pages and groups raised funds through Tshidz death under the guise of raising these monies to assist with the funeral.

While social media is often seen as the highlight reel of our lives, there are instances in which people can get pretty deep and vulnerable with what they choose to share. As social media has evolved, so have our public displays of grief. From entire photo albums to heartfelt posts to carefully crafted video montages, our compulsion to share remains the same, but our feeds seem to play a role in shaping how we memorialise those we've lost.

When we post on social media about our loved ones who died, we are allowing other people to be able to witness our grief.

In many ways, this new approach has become the norm. Plenty of people especially the young now turn to social media while grieving to memorialise and remember what they loved about the person they lost, and to share the memories that they still hold onto. Far from being unusual, sharing in this way may actually be vital to the grieving process. I remember reading something to this effect from author and speaker, David Kessler, he said that grief needs to be witnessed to be healed. I couldn't agree more with that.

9

Grief and loneliness

Lonely
I think of you in the morning
before the sun rises,
when in the still of the darkness
my heart feels your presence.
Though you are gone to a better place
Memories of Your love, your tenderness,
your slow rhythmic breathing as you sleep, still fill my heart
and I am at peace.

I think of you when the first rays of sunlight
spill like a waterfall between the blinds
and settle in my eyes.
I know and I am fast accepting that
I cannot reach my hand, my foot, or any body part physically, but my soul still feels your touch.
Your memories feed my heart, my soul, my spirit,
and I am at peace.

I think of you at noon when the sun is at its highest,
when the heat warms my skin
and causes my eyes to close with sheer pleasure.
Thoughts of you surround me, envelop me, overpower me.
Images of you swirl around like a funnel cloud,
sucking into its grasp all that it touches,
and I am at peace.

I think of you when the sun is setting
and its final rays of light begin to fade.
I can hear your voice, sweet, soft, and slow in my head –
words of beauty, joy, friendship, and everlasting love.
My heart begins to sing a love song so sweet and so gentle.
I still go to the gym and walk the places that together we once walked.
And I am at peace.

I think of you when the sun has set and the stillness of the moon
is displaying one of its many wondrous phases.
Thoughts of your smile, your laugh, and your eyes
create a feeling that is impossible to express with just words.
The need to touch you, to feel you, to walk with you, share a joke
with you, is a need I can no longer physically fulfil. But,
I am at peace.

The intersection of grief and loneliness is complicated. Though loneliness, as a concept, is one I think many assume we understand.

We equate loneliness to the very definable concept of being alone, which means "without other people," and thanks to "lonely people" archetypes – like the spinsters with ten cats and misunderstood teenagers – we think we have a good idea of how loneliness looks.

People can feel alone in a crowd, a small group, a conversation, a family, or even a party. Loneliness strikes when we feel misunderstood, judged, or belittled. It creeps in when we sense our hearts are at a different place from those around us.

The trouble is that loneliness is subjective, so there's no way anyone can truly know what it looks like.

In the *Encyclopaedia of Mental Health (1998)* researchers, Daniel Perlman and Letita Anne Peplau define loneliness as,

"The subjective psychological discomfort people experience when their network of social relationships is significantly deficient in either quality or quantity."

In other words, loneliness occurs when a person's social relationships don't meet their interpersonal needs or desires. I find the definition given above very informative it says nothing about the state of being alone. Instead, that loneliness is a feeling of discomfort that arises when a person subjectively feels unfulfilled by their social relationships.

Loss shakes us. The mind spins, while the heart frantically searches for solid ground in the midst of what feels like a free fall. The loneliness that comes from grieving can be felt even when you are surrounded by friends. In the time soon after Tshidz death I missed her even more when I was around our mutual friends.

There was that loneliness that of missing someone you wish was there, but you know they are gone forever, nonetheless the feeling persists.

If you're grieving, you may feel this has become the story of your life. There are aspects of grief that make loneliness seem inevitable and unsolvable. Primarily, the fact that what you desire is your loved one, and what you have is an emptiness moulded so precisely to your loved one's likeness that no one else could ever fill it.

Tshidz had an awkward sense of humour, I understood her timing and off timing at times with regards jokes. And so, over the years we had perfected our communication we could communicate verbally and nonverbally, we had inside jokes and in truth I've come to understand that loneliness after the death of a loved one is many things. Above all else, it's the ache of having loved someone so much that pieces of you became them, and pieces of them became you.

When Tshidz left this Earth, she took pieces of our shared life with her, and without her my life felt incomplete.

I can honestly say that I lost one of the few people in this world who really truly "got" me.

I am still in the process of solving loneliness caused by grief. It takes time and effort. It takes changing those moments and memories that made you sad into moments you celebrate and cherish. For a long time, I found activities that I did with Tshidz such as walking or hiking up the hills difficult to do on my own, these activities reminded me so much of her and brought sad emotions.

Where does your pain emanate from?

A family can experience a loss together, yet all of them still feel alone. Part of this is natural, because the loss is different for each person. No one fully understands another's thoughts or emotions.

Looking at my experience with the loss and the process of grieving Tshidz, I realised my pain was emanating from a different source from that which my son's pain originated.

I lost a wife, and my son lost his mother. The mother child connection is more than emotional it is a soul connection from the womb, 'conception connection'. I believe every woman and yes, I am saying every woman feels an overwhelming unconditional love for her unborn child as he or she grows in the womb. Some people say that it is because of hormones or a mother's intuition and yes both can play a role in the way a woman feels while she is pregnant, but it is not the only contributing factor as why this deep connection on a soul level occurs. There is a bond between mother and child that grows just as deep and intimate as a bond between husband and wife or soulmates.

The connection between mother and child is so precious and unique that it is felt by both mother and child throughout their lifetime. The mother's soul and that of the child are bound together in oneness in the most intimately possible way that two souls can ever come together, and the energy of this bond will last and be remembered on a soul level forever. It can never be undone or forgotten. I can never fully comprehend what my son was going through, I know his loss is huge and all I can do is to be as supportive as I can be, and always be there for him.

The bond I had with Tshidz was that of love, we had a very healthy love relationship. Losing my wife brought about many unexpected changes. A wife or partner is someone extremely close and indeed the loss brings with it other secondary losses which impact on not only your life but, the lives of other surviving family members. The grieve felt from the loss of a loved one is not homogeneous, the personal experience of loss should be looked at individually, as no two people will be impacted in the same way.

When Tshidz died, I felt I had lost my hopes and dreams, we shared hopes and dreams we had the same vision, and she was my partner in that walk to achieve these aspirations. We had planned a future together, we had dreams of travelling together in our twilight years. Losing hopes and dreams is such a devastating and heart wrenching feeling, but it is only a secondary feeling of loss. Having that loved one absent in your life is a loss that words cannot explain.

I questioned my faith, and by God I was on the brink of completely losing my faith after her death. My mind was flooded with questions; "Why would God do this to me?" "Why would a loving God take away a mother from my young son?"

Losing a spouse, a wife in my case felt like losing a better part of myself. I did not feel whole as I felt that my better half was gone forever. I felt for a long while like a grain of rice abandoned in the desert. I had to learn new roles, I had to adapt to life without Tshidz.

Amidst all the mourning and grieving the feeling of loneliness would grip and overwhelm me, losing a loved one can result in social losses because some people find relating to someone who is grieving quite difficult and therefore step back or avoid interacting with you. I experienced this social loss and it left me feeling isolated and alone. In-laws and some of Tshidz's friends had already distanced themselves from me following the outrageous allegations and rumours that they had pedalled with regards poisoning (the Polonium 2-10) which I had supposedly accrued in Russia.

Losing someone you love can be like losing one half of yourself. The pain and emptiness felt during the grieving process can go on for months or years, however no two people will ever respond to the same situation in the same way. Working through grief is a day by day, week by week process. You may have bad days when you think you will never recover from this loss. You may also think that you will never function successfully without this person in your life. The good news is that you will recover, and you will be fully functional, if you choose to.

Each one of us changes in some way after the death of someone we love. Some of us may harden after the experience; some will soften, but those who choose to learn and grow from this tragic time, will go on with their life remembering 'what was' and appreciating 'what is'.

Grief is lonely. Because life is about relationships and we're all relational creatures, we don't typically deal well with the pain of separation. Loneliness is not one of our goals in life.

If you're grieving, most likely, you're struggling with the pain of loneliness. You don't need people to try and fix it or make this better. They can't. But wouldn't it be great if a few were aware of your pain and supported you when the loneliness hit?

Pain is natural part of grief and healing. We need safe people who will accept us where we are and be with us in this. As others accept us, we just might be able to accept ourselves.

Lonely? Yes. That's a part of grief.

Alone? Never. The lonely road of grief is well populated. We're in this together.

Lessons learnt

Loss of companionship

If you lived with the person who died you might now find

yourself living alone, perhaps for the first time. Even with lots of friends and family visiting it can be hard to adapt. It's normal to miss someone just being around. I often would find myself saying or thinking I miss someone to do nothing with, indeed there are times I missed just doing nothing with Tshidz but was comforted by just being in her presence doing absolutely nothing.

Loss of connections

When someone dies you might also lose connections with the people you knew through them. Perhaps they were the one who organised your social life, or you often spent time with their friends or family. A death can put a strain on these types of relationships.

Lack of invitations

Sometimes invitations can dry up after a death. You might find that soon after the funeral support and sympathy seem to run out. It might feel like those around you have stopped making a special effort. If you previously socialised as a couple, as a family or as a group of friends, you might now feel like it's difficult to return to social events alone.

Losing friends

It is a sad fact that people do lose friends when someone dies. People feel awkward about reaching out and can even stop making contact all together.

If you were caring for the person who died, it might now have been a long time since you've been able to socialise in the usual way. Caring for others can be a lonely experience in itself. But when the caring role ends it can also leave a big gap, with many hours to fill which were previously spent looking after someone else.

Grief can feel lonely

Even if you have lots of people around you, grief can still make you feel lonely. Someone has died that you had a unique connection with, and it can be hard for other people to understand what you're going through. This is often made worse if the death was very traumatic. If you are younger, you might be one of the only people your age to have experienced this type of loss. It might feel like nobody else understands.

What can help?

Reaching out, can help. Sometimes it just takes one person making the first step to rebuild lost connections. Try contacting those who were in your life before you were bereaved.

10

Questioning my religion

Where is God, I grieve
My life is full of grieving,
tears of agony … The loss of loved one
Death is never easy
My father, my brother, my sister, my mother…
Now my wife, my life is a cycle of misery.
sorrow's clouds, continuously
hanging over me
Where is God?
My Life is full of weeping,
sobs so ever mournful
Trying my best not to question but my mind is failing
I am grieving forever grieving
Sorrow's clouds pouring grief season after season.
My Life is punctuated by weeping,
cries of distress . . .
but joy comes to those
who into Christ press!
So, they say but I have pressed yet I still grieve.
Am I wrong to question?
Why? Where? When will this stop?

Getting angry with God and questioning your faith after your loved one's death is normal as part of the struggle to make sense of their death.

No doubt religion can be incredibly comforting at times of loss, especially when you feel devastated and broken inside. But it can also leave you confused with a profound sense of emptiness when your beliefs can't help you acknowledge or accept your loss.

I questioned my believes and religion a lot and re-examined some of my once strongly held views after Tshidz's death.

Indeed, blaming God or questioning your faith after the death of someone you love is arguably a natural reaction to grief. It's normal for people to go through spiritual trials after suffering loss, questioning their faith, and going through denial and anger at God as they try to reconcile their grief.

Grief can cause you to confuse your feelings toward your faith and religion as the death of your loved one brings about a crisis of faith.

I am a Christian convert, one of the first in my family to actively practice Christianity my immediate family believed in a Christian God, but they were mostly inactive and occasionally visited church.

My father had a massive Bible in the house which he would occasionally make us read when I was younger.

I joined a church when I was 18 and became a missionary in The Church of Jesus Christ of the Latter-Day Saints. A church in which my older brother and mother later joined.

I gained and formed many friendships with Christians that have persisted to this day.

However, I left the church in my 30's and joined a number of other churches since then.

I believed, I had a strong anchor in Christ and that my faith was unshakable.

I went through a lot of grieving from the death of my father, my young brother my elder sister and that of my mother and in all that my anchor in Christ and my faith in Christianity held strong. I managed to pull through without questioning my faith.

But the death of my wife shook me to the core. I was angry, I questioned God's love and it altered the way I looked at everything.

My well-intentioned Christian friends and pastors rallied behind me trying best they could to strengthen me, to cement my faith.

But unbeknown to them some of the damage was from the words they said. They threw little quips at me when I was grieving, aimed at helping me 'move on.'

Words that were meant to comfort and strength became the source of my confusion and disgruntlement.

"Those who believe need not grieve."

Needless to say, I felt some frustration and conflict about such quips and comment. As I was writing this book, I considered what the source of this anecdote might be, and it seems it could be connected to the Bible passage 1 Thessalonians 4:13:

> *"Brothers and sisters, we do not want you to be uninformed about those who sleep in death, so that you do not grieve like the rest of mankind, who have no hope."*

I questioned this phrase, its oversimplification of grief and faith can undoubtedly cause pain to grievers and hence after Tshidz's death I took umbrage, I questioned my faith, I wondered if there was a God and if he indeed cared?

Religion and spirituality are complex but important topics in the wake of a loss. Christianity can be an incredible comfort in times of loss. But losses can also cause you to question your faith, as you struggle to make sense of the death. Grief can confuse our feelings about our faith… and our faith can confuse feelings about our grief.

There's a separate discussion to be had about those who grieve without belief in God or an afterlife, but it suffices to say: People of faith don't always accept their losses quietly and calmly. A faithful person's heartaches and pains hurt them just as much as someone who doesn't count on spirituality or religion in their lives. When someone you love dies, grief is a natural reaction to loss no matter what you believe in.

I have absolutely no doubt that – in nearly every case the expression 'Those who believe need not grieve' is uttered – it is with the best of intentions. Just like, "He's in a better place" or "It's all part of God's plan," these platitudes are shared with the hope that they will bring comfort to the griever.

What became complicated for me was when I internalised these quotes and started to feel that the depth of my grief was somehow reflective of my faith.

This left me questioning why I was still feeling the pain of grief when someone I loved was now with God.

Grief was my natural reaction to the loss of my wife.

I felt a deep and aching pain when Tshidz died. I felt the dozens of emotions that come with grief: sadness, anger, guilt, fear, loneliness, blame, and much more. Though faith that someone is in a better place or that you will see them again can be a comfort, this does not remove the pain that the person is gone. It does not change the trauma that can come from watching someone suffer from a prolonged or painful illness. This does not eliminate the anger, blame, guilt, regret, or countless other feelings that can come up following a death.

It is not that your grief and your faith should be separate. It's that you must remember that the depth of your grief does not imply a loss of faith. The problem with the statement "Those who believe need not grieve" is that one is made to feel that the reverse must be true: Those who do grieve do not believe.

My hope is that by sharing my lived experiences with grieving those who are going through grieving, and perhaps feel that their faith should be enough to eliminate their grief, please understand and learn this:

Experiencing grief DOES NOT indicate a loss of faith.

Let me say it one more time: Experiencing grief DOES NOT indicate a loss of faith.

When a person of deep faith loses someone, it's important to remember that grief is about their own experience of loss. It's perfectly reasonable for someone to believe that their loved one is in a better place, and still to feel overwhelmed with the pain of being separated from them. Furthermore, a person can believe in a greater plan – all while still experiencing the pain of absence. It's not selfish to grieve, and it's definitely not a loss of faith. It's a normal reaction to a devastating situation that can coexist with the comfort of one's faith and spirituality.

Faith communities should be a place of comfort and support in times of loss. Thankfully, for many they are. But then again not every faith community brings this support. In fact, some bring judgment and criticism for the emotions of grief, fixating on the idea that grief and faith cannot coexist. This leaves grievers feeling as though their grief has been minimized or misunderstood. If you have felt this way, I encourage you to consider that grieving the separation from someone you love can exist along with a faith that they are in a better place and that you will see them again.

You don't need anyone's permission to grieve. Don't let anyone tell you otherwise! It is so important to find the people and place that allow you to grieve however long you want. Grieving is not an event it is a process.

I remember as the one-year anniversary of Tshidz's death approached, I was taken aback by some subtle and not-so-subtle comments indicating that perhaps my son and I should be ready to "move on." The soft, compassionate cocoon that had enveloped us months before had lulled me into believing others would be patient with us on our grief journey, and while I'm sure many will read this and quickly say "Take all the time you need," I'm increasingly aware that the cocoon may be in the process of collapsing. It's understandable when you take a step back. I mean, life goes on. The hundreds who supported us in the aftermath of Tshidz death wept and mourned with us, prayed passionately for us, and sent an unbelievable volume of cards, letters, emails, texts, phone calls, and gifts. The support was utterly amazing. But for most, life never stopped – their world didn't grind to a horrific, catastrophic halt on May 29, 2019. In fact, their lives have kept moving steadily forward with tasks, routines, work, kids, leisure, plans, dreams, goals etc. LIFE GOES ON. And some of them are ready for us to go on too. They want the old Brill and Trav back.

They secretly wonder when things will get back to normal for us – when we'll be ourselves, when the tragedy of Tshidz's death will cease to be the grid that we pass everything across. And I have to tell you – the old Brill and Trav are gone. They're never coming back. We will never be the same again. There is a new "normal." 29 May 2019 has permanently marked us. It will remain the grid we pass everything across for an indeterminate amount of time… maybe forever.

Because these comments from well-meaning folks wounded me so deeply, I doubted myself and thought perhaps I really am not grieving "well" (whatever that means). I wondered if I was being overly sensitive

People can be so rude and insensitive; they make the most thoughtless comments," one grieving father said. You know, it wasn't all that long ago that it was standard in our culture for people to officially be in mourning for a full year. They wore black. They didn't go to parties. They didn't smile a whole lot. And everybody accepted their period of mourning; no one ridiculed a mother in black or asked her stupid questions about why she was STILL so sad. Obviously, this is no longer accepted practice; mourners are encouraged to quickly move on, turn the corner, get back to work, think of the positive, be grateful for what is left, and other unkind, unfeeling, obtuse and downright cruel comments. What does this say about us – other than we're terribly uncomfortable with death, with grief, with mourning, with loss – or we're so self-absorbed that we easily forget the profound suffering the loss of a wife creates in the shattered husband and remaining child.

Unless you've stood by the bedside of your wife and watched her take her last breath, you're better off keeping your words to some very simple phrases: "I'm so sorry for your loss." Or "I'm praying for you and your family." Do your best to avoid the meaningless, catch-all phrase "How are you doing?" This question is almost impossible to answer. If you're a stranger, it's none of your business. If you're a casual acquaintance, it's excruciating to try to answer honestly, and you leave the sufferer unsure whether to lie to you (I'm ok) to end the conversation or if they should try to haltingly tell you that their right arm was cut off and they don't know how to go on without it. If you're a close friend, try telling them instead, "You don't have to say anything at all; I'm with you in this."

Don't be the pseudo comforter who drives a griever mad with questions, wrong conclusions and assumptions about their grief. Say nothing if you have no good and constructive words. The pseudo comforter often fills the uncomfortable silence with words that wound rather than heal. It is sad and somewhat empathy deprived to see how pseudo comforters are insensitive to a griever's shattering loss – They can be callous with the grief of another and rush through the conversation without really listening, blithely spouting the platitudes such as 'it's not the end of the world, you will be fine, you will need to move on'.

Here's my plea: Please don't ever tell someone 'They need to move on' allow them a chance to mourn what they've lost. It will take longer than you think is reasonable, rational or even right. But that's ok. True friends – unlike pseudo comforters – love at all times, and brothers and sisters are born to help in time of need (Prov. 17:17 LB). The truest friends and "helpers" are those who wait for the griever to emerge from the darkness that swallowed them alive without growing afraid, anxious or impatient. They don't pressure their friend to be the old familiar person they're used to; they're willing to accept that things are different, embrace the now scarred one they love, and are confident that their compassionate, non-demanding presence is the surest expression of God's mercy to their suffering friend. They're ok with messy and slow and few answers … and they never say, "Move on."

The experience of questioning my faith and religion particularly during my grieving journey taught me some important lessons. One of the most important things at this time is to be kind to yourself and avoid getting tied up in knots trying to work out what you "really" believe. If it's unclear for a while, try to be patient and go with the uncertainty, and the answer may become clearer.

Realise that what you're experiencing is similar to bereavement, so allow yourself to grieve for what you've lost. Even if you're thinking "how could I have been so blind?", remember that it is something that previously meant a lot to you and provided stability. Bear in mind the major stages of grieving: denial, anger, bargaining, depression and acceptance.

I found that sharing my feelings with a compassionate and trustworthy person who understood my disillusionment and doubts and did not impose their own beliefs on me was very helpful.

I would advise that during this time you should try not to "rebound" towards an alternative belief system straight away, to fill the gap. Give yourself time to re-evaluate your needs. You are now opened to thinking new thoughts and doing new things. This can feel very liberating.

You are not alone in your struggle. I believe that thousands of others have felt the same way as you. Experiencing periods of doubt is actually a healthy process and much better than avoiding the issue or pushing it down. And ultimately, you will be better equipped to help someone else going through the same process.

11

My Dance with Alcohol and Grief

While alcohol can feel like an easy relief, the truth is that alcohol can actually perpetuate your grief. After, learning of Tshidz's cancer and after receiving her prognosis, I went into mourning. The cancer specialist that was taking care of her had broken the news that she had about three or so months to live.

I was in denial, I found it difficult to sleep and alcohol became my depressant.

Research has shown that intake of alcohol slows the central nervous system and brain making it harder for one to process their emotions and can leave their feelings unresolved.

Indeed, alcohol and grief have a tragic, and all-too-common, relationship. When a loved one passes away, the fallout can be devastating. I took to strong drink months before and after Tshidz death.

I was deeply impacted by her loss. Grief is a response to that loss and can sometimes be overwhelming, especially when the person lost was an integral part of another's life.

Alcohol is very present in our modern world. Between bars, liquor stores, and parties, we are constantly surrounded by the substance. Even at funerals, it is common to toast to the recently departed as a way to show respect. This, however, can be the steppingstone to developing a larger issue down the road.

People come to term with loss in many different ways. In

some cases, that can lead them to start using alcohol. It is one thing to drink alcohol recreationally. Someone could go for years drinking modestly without developing a problem, but once they start drinking for a specific reason, be it grief, depression, or even anger, they can easily fall down a rabbit hole of abuse.

It is far too common in today's world for people to drink after some kind of negative feeling as a way to take the edge off. It's easy to rationalise that a drink after experiencing a loss such as the death of a loved one can help someone relax and even go to sleep. However, once someone starts drinking in this way, it makes them more likely to form a habit of it. That habit may start out innocent enough, who would take a drink away from someone in mourning, it is that reliance on it that makes people require more to get the same effect. Eventually, this tolerance they've built can become a dependence.

I was falling deep into the proverbial rabbit hole; Jameson whiskey was constantly at my side.

Indeed, a few shots of the Irish whiskey felt like an easy relief, the truth is that with each shot and bottle of alcohol I actually perpetuate my grief. This is because alcohol functions as a depressant in the body, slowing the central nervous system and brain. This made it harder for me to process my emotions and in truth it left the pain of grieving unresolved.

Grief, no matter how bad it may seem, does pass via the use of alcohol. I was using alcohol as a band-aid, it was like trying to repair a foundation with duct tape. I was in a dangerous place psychologically and mentally I realised that alcohol is not medication, and it definitely isn't therapeutic. It is a drug. It provided temporary relief for a much deeper issue. While it may seem like it helps in the short term, using it as a crutch was only creating a bigger, longer-lasting problem. I had to deal with my grief minus the alcohol.

Many people turn to alcohol when coping with grief, stemming from watching a loved one go through a terminal illness and pass on.

Losing Tshidz was definitely one of the most upsetting and painful experiences I have gone through. I went through a wide range of emotions, from anger and denial to sadness and despair. I understand now more than ever before that each person goes through the grieving process differently, and they don't always do it in the healthiest manner. Some turn to alcohol in an attempt to numb the sadness, pain, and grief that follows a major loss such as the death of a parent, spouse, or child.

Sadly, self-medicating all that emotional pain often leads to alcohol addiction, with grief's impact on mental health taking a serious toll – even for the seemingly strongest and most resilient individuals. During the grieving process, it's critical that you experience and express emotions so that you can eventually move on with life and heal. However, some people get stuck as they begin struggling with unresolved grief, which is basically grief that lasts longer than normal.

I remember one night in my drunken stupor, calling my special friend (a medical professional) who had become the person that I would speak to and express my grief to, I was in a very bad place mentally. She was so concerned at the things I said. I don't quite remember what I said to her but that triggered her into action, and she stepped up to help me fight alcohol and that was how I got out of that rabbit hole into which I was falling deeper and deeper into.

While the reasons not to drink were well-known, to me I

had still participated in this self-destructive behaviour. It was the conversation that I had with my friend that made me review not only the impact of abusing alcohol, but how it specifically affected my healing from loss and grief:

I comprehend then, that Alcohol impacted on my sleep: contrary to a view held by some people that when one drinks before bed, they get a better night's sleep. The truth is the quality of the sleep that happens when impaired just isn't the same.

Not only was I not getting the right kind of sleep after drinking, but I was likely to wake up even more tired and hurting than I was before.

Sleep is one of the most important tools for physically and mentally healing each day, and every care should be taken not to hamper the sleep that can elude so many.

I also reflected on the things I said and the way I acted when drunk anyone who has been around drinkers knows there's a lot of different types of "drunk". The happy drunk, the sad drunk, or perhaps the normally mild-mannered person who becomes aggressive or even mean when they drink.

I was all of these, I was ashamed of who I had become. It's important to remember that grieving is a time of self-discovery. I was trying to figure out who I was without Tshidz, adding this other facet to my confusion (even temporarily) made it very confusing for me and for those around me to know who I was and who I was evolving in to. A clear head and consistent behaviour are a necessary part of this journey, as is time for clarity and introspection.

I was fortunate to have friends that don't drink. My special friend (the medical practitioner)

Had a clear sense of how I really was doing. More importantly, she was always upfront and candid about my health and lifestyle at that moment.

This meant that I benefited from meaningful conversation that I had with her. I am grateful for this sober friend because had I been in the company of a non-sober person or if the times, I socialised were with other alcohol drinkers there were possibilities that this would have adversely affected me, and I would have possible felt as lonely as if I wasn't spending time with anyone at all.

Conversely, alcohol can keep people home. For some, a quiet night at home drinking can be much more appealing than going out. Those who are abusing alcohol may choose to forgo non-alcohol related activities (like the movies, for example), to drink at home alone. Relationships can be seriously affected when someone who has had a loss chooses alcohol over friends and family, and outlets for support can quickly diminish when a drink is chosen instead.

Research shows that grieving men are at particularly high risk for alcohol-related problems. In one study, men bereaved for one year and men bereaved for two years scored higher on multiple dimensions of dependence symptoms and harmful alcohol use than non-bereaved men. Bereaved men also have higher morbidity and mortality rates, potentially linked to their alcohol consumption.

Why do the struggles that men have with grief and alcohol appear more severe than women's struggles? Cultural expectations about masculinity may be the culprit. Men are often discouraged from showing their emotions. Drinking through their grief is sometimes seen as more masculine than grieving.

It takes courage and strength to tackle the feelings associated with loss head on. Grieving is a deeply human emotion, not a male or female trait. For any person, the best approach to grief is to feel it and process it without trying to numb the pain. As scary and overwhelming as grieving can be, the only way to get to the other side is to allow yourself to go through it.

12

Let the tears flow; cry if you must

It's so hard not to Cry,
I wasn't ready to let go,
They comfort me with words, saying you are now in a better place,
But what do I do in this bitter place?
Without you I feel out of place,
Memories bitter and sweet now fill up the empty space,
I will always remember your smiling face
I have it sketched in my heart and mind forever your space
It's so hard not to cry,
I wasn't ready to let go
Though they say you are in a better place
I would have preferred you here with me, sharing this space
Where we speak face to face
It's hard not to cry
Rest in peace
They say you are in a better place.

"The most painful goodbyes are the ones never said or never explained"

I have dealt with a lot of grieve in my life and each loss of a loved one has affected me in a different way. The death of my father, then the death of my young brother and again my sister and that of my mother were all sudden deaths, without sickness or hospitalisation for me they were goodbyes that never were. They were sudden life changing moments that brought grieving.

However, my wife's death was different she succumbed to cancer, and that brought with it grieve that was complicated. There was an anticipation of a pending death, nonetheless, the impact of death still remains something one can never fully prepare for. The grieving process is not something mechanical it is a fireball of emotions that one can never be ready for or fully prepare for. You simply don't know what the emotions and the grieving will bring.

I was beside her hospital bed at that moment she took her last breath. I could not cry at that precise moment, even when the doctors gave me time with her moments after her passing.

Tears might come as a simple moistening in the eyes, or gently fall while experiencing another's pain. They might come quite suddenly in a joyful moment, and we feel our heart burst open. I have often heard people saying tears are cleansing. Some that I have spoken to say that they would feel cleansed after a deep cry.

There are tears after a profound loss that can feel as if we will drown. There are also the tears after humiliation, betrayal, standing up for yourself when all you want is to be angry and confront, and then out pour the tears. Then that feels humiliating. Sometimes tears come after prolonged laugher, the kissin' cousin of tears, with at times moving into the weeping of deep pain that had been buried or ignored. It can feel as if we have no control, and we don't. Not really. We can make ourselves cry but that takes some practice and may be a surface experience only. We can at times hold our tears back, bite them back, but then everything else gets all scrunched up and we tighten around the tears or the loss. We can feel like we have not cried at the appropriate time, like at a funeral. Then, a few weeks later, we are watching a Hallmark commercial or a movie or listening to a song and the tears flow, sometimes gently and at times into a sob. We may not find tears at all in a loss experience as our primary feeling might be gratitude or relief.

The tears after profound loss don't necessarily flow freely. Not for me anyway. After I witnessed my wife take her last breath, I was in shock, and I was numb. I remember getting the call to rush to the hospital, they told me my wife situation had seriously deteriorated the doctor on the other end of the phone said "Make your way to the hospital it's not looking good" I did not tell my son what was going on I just said I needed to get to the hospital to be with his mother I would be back as soon as I can. Earlier that same day my wife had called her cousin and asked her to sleep over that night. I left My son with his aunt and rushed to the hospital, when I got there, I went to the hospital room that I had left her in earlier that evening, but she had been moved. A doctor came to that room and took me to the theatre where they were trying to resuscitate her and, on the way, there, one of the doctors who had called me to come the hospital/theatre rooms told me that she was in a very bad state "her major organs are shutting down, they are failing" he said.

I did not panic. I was numb. Then I saw her surrounded by all these doctors and nurses, they were trying to get her to breathe. As I walked in the lead doctor announced the time, I knew that was the time of her death. It was surreal it was as if time froze, I was allowed a few moments with her soon after that. I held her hand she looked like she had just fallen asleep. I had seen her suffering, and at that moment she looked so at peace she looked relieved free of pain.

I spent about 10 or so minutes, before the nurses and doctors that had attended to her came and took me out, I was offered condolences and offered tea, water and asked if I wanted to have a few moments to talk to a counsellor. I was not interested in any of that at that moment. My concern was now getting to my son and breaking this sad news to him.

I went into action. There was funeral planning, a eulogy to write, family arrangements, making sure her mother was informed and getting arrangements for her to come over to England. She would have wanted her to be there, God knows I wanted her to be present and for her to pay her last respects to her only daughter.

The period following Tshidz's death was hectic, it was stressful it was hell. The relationship that I had with my mother-in-law was not the best, yes. Nonetheless I had not envisaged that things would spiral into the chaotic mess that ensued in the aftermath of Tshidz's death.

Tshidz was a peaceful person she loved family and promoted love and unity in almost all situations. I had hoped that common-sense would prevail and those of us grieving her loss would unite and grant her a befitting funeral and send off. Her legacy of love and family unity demanded this from us.

But that was not to be, the events that followed became so ugly, the skirmishes soiled her otherwise beautiful legacy, making it even more painful to grieve and mourn.

I took a huge knock health-wise, emotionally and psychologically. It took a few weeks, and seeing I was not eating and sleeping at all, for me to realise and known that the pain was being held in too long and I needed to mourn and grieve, I needed to let out the tears I had been supressing.

Not having tears does not have to mean one is numb. It does not necessarily mean the heart is closed. The mantra from my childhood goes, "Big boys don't cry." It has been hard for me to fully cry in another's presence. I have had to learn to trust that experience as it does not come naturally. Cultural differences also play a huge factor in how we express grief. I knew I had to work at having the funeral concluded. I had to make sure she was buried and to get that done in a respectful and dignified way. I supressed most of my emotions to allow me to power on and arrange all that was needed to make this happen. Her immediate family became antagonistic they refused to cooperate and chose to boycott the funeral. It was very sad; it was confusing for my son. It complicated an already painful situation. But that's what grieving does, at times it makes people become extremely irrational. They chose to take out whatever pain Tshidz's death had brought to them on us.

I had become the focal point to direct all that anger, I was going through hell. I had lost a wife, a companion with whom I had shared 20 years of my life. I had lived with her for half her life. She died at the age of 40.

It was a while after my wife's passing that I met a special friend who taught to be open with my emotions. To this day I marvel at how peaceful I felt whenever I was around her and how tears could flow naturally and freely in pain or joy. I never felt judged, but just loved around her. I treasured her free open expression and realised how the witnessing of her genuine love and her own tears opened my heart. My heart was full of supressed tears, I had so much pain that had been held back. I had no way of letting it out. I had due to cultural reasons held back tears that needed to come out.

Some cultures encourage and live out a very natural robust expression. For others it is stoic. We are a melting pot of an array of expressions, and we cannot judge one against the other. And certainly, we cannot judge ourselves in our experience. At best we bring compassion and curiosity.

I remember talking to my friend about the moment Tshidz passed on and telling her how much pain it brought to my heart and yet I couldn't cry at that moment. Upon reflection I often asked myself if it is okay not to cry as others do in moments like that which I went through. I have encountered this question in the past from friends and at times from myself. Tears are curious things. They can come unexpectedly, unwanted, in torrents, or gently and softly, and not at all. And then we wonder, why?

It is all okay. Tears are not required. Rather than, why am I not crying, I might ask; Is there something I am not expressing? What do I wish to express? In what way now do I want to express myself? Create? Build? Write? Sing? Laugh? In what way do I best express myself? Then, after the question, return to the heart and listen.

Tears are healing because they flow from the heart and there is a myriad of ways to express from the heart. When we do allow expression, we feel not only a deeper connection to self but to the greening world around us, to the collective whole, to sacred Oneness. In our honest open expression, we come to an inner silence, the doorway to the Divine.

13

Don't lose yourself to grieving

Every culture has its own set of beliefs that describe how the world works and people's roles in the world. In societies in which most people share the same religion, religious beliefs significantly shape the culture. Each culture has its own beliefs about the meaning and purpose of life and what happens after death. This informs how people in those cultures approach death. For example, people may find death more bearable if they believe in a life after death. In some cultures, people believe that the spirit of someone who has died directly influences the living family members. The family members are comforted by the belief that their loved one is watching over them. In general, beliefs about the meaning of death help people make sense of it and cope with its mystery.

Whether you are grieving the loss of a spouse, parent, child, sibling, friend or someone else close to you, please remember to take care of yourself.

GIVE YOURSELF PERMISSION TO GRIEVE

I personally come from a society which expects us to "be strong" and "carry on", nonetheless one needs to appreciate the fact that grief is quite needy. It consumes most of your energy and it demands your full attention at all times, whether you like it or not. The only way to move forward and adapt to life without your loved one is to give yourself permission to grieve.

If there is anything I have learnt from past experiences that I can share right here I would say, don't let others define your grief and tell you how you should feel.

When someone close to you dies people come to mourn with you and they do their best to comfort and console and condole with you. One most common thing that people do is they try to comfort you with words, the most common is *"time will heal you"* but is there truth to that? Does time really heal a grieving person?

In truth after suffering the loss of a loved one, one does not heal. After the loss of a loved one, we are never the same. The gap felt when one loses a mother, or a father can never be filled or erased by time. What we try to do is accept that there is now a void that can never be filled. There will always be moments that we will feel that gap/void and we will feel and miss and wish those we loved were present.

In different cultures and countries, people choose to grieve very differently. But there are many commonalities that unite us worldwide. Having a good cry is common throughout most of our cultural and religious traditions. Regardless of background, expressing grief can help us to process loss in meaningful ways.

People often adapt the beliefs and values of their culture to meet their unique needs and circumstances. As a result, grief responses within a culture vary from person to person. This is especially true in societies made up of people from many cultural backgrounds. A family with members from 2 or more cultural backgrounds may develop its own set of rituals and customs.

In some instances, a person's experience of grief may be at odds with cultural norms. For example, someone who is quiet and reserved may not feel comfortable crying in public as expected. Others may have a level of despair that feels out of step with cultural beliefs about life after death. Despite cultural norms, people need to grieve in ways that feel right to them.

It is important to attend to your physical needs during the period after a loss. Grieving is both emotionally and physically exhausting. Care for yourself by trying to get enough sleep at night, eating a healthy diet, and exercising.

LISTEN TO YOUR BODY

One of the key lessons I learnt from my experience was to listen to my body. It is very easy to stop caring for yourself while grieving. I neglected my body, but I had to pick myself up. Indeed, the human body is perfectly capable of letting you know what it needs and when. Listen to it and eat if you feel hungry, drink water if you are thirsty and sleep when you feel tired.

A year or so before Tshidz's dead she had got me into walking and had even signed me up at the local gym (she had paid up for my year's subscription even the year she passed on). I had got to understand then that exercising improves not just your physical but your mental health as well. When you exercise, your body produces endorphins which lift your mood and improve the way you feel. I can attest to the importance of exercise and its benefits, it helped me during my grieving. Another thing I got into was meditation, it helped me calm down and it was helpful in reducing the stress I was going through.

DON'T SUPRESS YOUR EMOTIONS

Like I have already stated it difficult for me to express some of my emotions and thus, I bottled up a lot. I have learnt from experience that pretending that you are okay when you are not, does not make grief disappear.

It is important to allow yourself to experience the pain of loss. As much as it hurts, it is natural and healthy to grieve. Sometimes people feel guilty about the way they feel, thinking they should "get over it." Let yourself grieve and fully experience your feelings, such as shock, sadness, anger, and loneliness. Don't judge yourself for any feelings you have, even if you think you shouldn't have them. Let yourself react in ways that help you process and release intense emotions, even if it means crying.

I personally learnt that I needed to go through the motions and find a healthy way of expressing my feelings. Talking to someone helps and so does grief counselling but if that's not the way you do things, then there are other ways to help you achieve the same result. Start a journal and write about your feelings and thoughts in it. That would help you to validate your grief and enable you to work though it in a healthy way.

DON'T ISOLATE YOURSELF

Admittedly there will be times that you need your space and want to be alone to process your thoughts and feelings, but do not completely isolate yourself.

Whilst wanting to withdraw from public life and restrict yourself to the boundaries of your own home is quite normal under the circumstances, you must make an effort to prevent it from becoming a habit. Interacting with others and spending time with those close to you are important parts of the healing process.

I found it helpful to talk about my loss and sadness with my special friend. It helped me process and release my feelings. I let my friend know that it can be helpful for me to share my feelings with her. And bless her because sometimes I would tell her the same story over and over. I reassured her that I did not expect her to have answers; I just wanted her to listen. She was very helpful through the most difficult times as she allowed me to think out loud which was what I needed at that time.

FAMILY AND FRIENDS

The period after Tshidz's burial was perhaps the most challenging for me. Everyone had gone back to carry-on with life as it were. I had busied myself with funeral arrangements and all the other things that needed to be done and that had sort of kept me occupied. I had not really noticed how much support I would need after.

Your family, friends and those close to you are your support network and you need to let them be there for you. Give them the chance to do what they can to make life easier for you at this difficult time. Don't let your pride and independence stay in the way and alienate them.

I don't really have family in the UK, I do however, have friends. I had a very dedicated 'mother' Mrs Chitsa (a family friend from Wolverhampton), she and her friends would come to check on my son and I, every Wednesday with no fail and they made sure they brought my son fruits and all the other goodies. She would come with; an uplifting message and her support and visits were extremely helpful and appreciated. I can never thank her enough.

My lesson from experience was: Be proactive and reach out to family and friends during times such as mourning or grieving. If appropriate, involve them in the funeral planning process, ask for second opinion on decisions you need to make etc. Let them know that they are an important part of your life.

GIVE YOURSELF A BREAK

Give yourself a break from grieving. It is healthy to take breaks from grieving with pleasant activities and interactions with supportive family members and friends. People need a break from the pain of grieving. Part of adapting to a loss is to go back and forth between focusing on the loss and finding a way to be in the world without the person you lost. For example, you might choose to go to dinner with friends, take a relaxing bath, watch a movie, start a new hobby, or enjoy the outdoors. It is good for you to enjoy yourself and okay to laugh and feel happy, despite your loss.

SUCCESSFUL MOURNING

Mourning is the process by which bereaved people seek and find ways to turn the light on in the world again. From a clinical perspective, mourning is an array of psychological processes that can be roughly grouped as emotion regulation and learning processes. When successful, mourning leads people to feel deeply connected to deceased loved ones while also able to imagine a satisfying future without them. After mourning successfully, a bereaved person is re-engaged in daily life, reconnected to others, and able to experience hope for a future with potential for joy and satisfaction. Grief has been transformed and integrated. A successful mourning process entails effective emotion regulation and assimilation of new learning in long-term memory.

Our loved ones exist in long-term memory, but there are different kinds of memory. Episodic, semantic, and implicit memory are inter-related but serve different functions, entail different brain systems, and have different properties. Close attachments are mapped in each of these systems, so each must be updated when a loved one dies. To update explicit memory means learning new stories and facts. To update semantic memory means learning new meanings and rules, and to update implicit memory means extinguishing conditioned reward responses and learning new motor patterns and other procedural responses that are permanently out of awareness. Given this multifaceted goal, it makes sense that mourning is a complex process that is often lengthy and arduous. We must repeatedly engage with information about the death and its myriad consequences in order to adequately assimilate it and amend existing information about the deceased in each memory system.

One of the challenges of mourning is that the required learning is both intensely emotional and deeply aversive. Awareness of mortality registers in a specific area of our brains and almost always registers as a threat. We naturally resist thinking of our own death and even more so that of our loved ones. We must overcome this resistance in order to confront and assimilate the information that a loved one is gone. When we do confront the reality, we are often assailed by tidal waves of negative emotion. Grief can overwhelm our usual emotion regulation capacity, forcing us to resort to escape and avoidance to get some respite.

14

Gossipers and acquaintances show up for different reasons

They came like owls
wild-eyed, nocturnal fowl,
Rotating heads
Etching ears
gossips looking to talk
traitor's scheming,
And jealous fiends on evil bent,
With ignoble vices unredeeming,
Not here to comfort those mourning
But looking for gossip to spread in the morning
Trash and tarnish the names of the innocent.
Extinguishing hope by magnifying the grievers sorrow,
The future dim and cloudy lies today
they brew and broadcast tomorrow
Though gossiper's tales bring tears of sorrow that dim the eyes.
Cheer up, take courage, do not falter,
Truth will triumph by and by,
Time all evil things will alter,
Vice and wickedness will soon be exposed let the sun rise look up
As light appears all darkness will disappear.

Tshidz had always spoken so passionately about her school days. She went to a girl's school Usher Institute a school established by the Salvation Army Church at Leighwoods farm near Figtree, just outside her hometown Bulawayo in Zimbabwe.

She spoke of her experiences there and how they made a tough woman out her.

She spoke of the friends she made there, she had many friends some of them good and others very bad.

She had warned me about the culture of gossip amongst the girls from Usher nonetheless she kept contact with a lot of her school friends.

When she died a lot of her school friends who are U.K. based reached out to pass condolences and some came to the house and others attended the funeral.

But most of those who came to the house had ulterior motives, they were looking for gossip.

They created their own versions of what had transpired. Tshidz had not divulge her fight with cancer thusly, most of those who claimed to know her had no clue what her cause of death was.

This vacuum created space for gossipers to try and fill in the blanks and as such many untruths and falsehoods were created and shared.

All of a sudden some 'Usher-girls' became cancer experts. A lot was said about how healthy she looked, how this could not have been cancer because her hair did not fall out. How can one die from cancer in a developed country such as England?

How come she did not get chemotherapy?

A lot of the things said by these gossipers only displayed their ignorance.

I remember welcoming one lady into our home who said

she was Tshidz's friend and former head girl at school. She came with her two kids.

I had just dropped of my son at his dance class I had tried to tell her I was busy because at that time I just needed some alone time. But she kept calling to ask if she could come and pass her condolences in person, she said she was visiting with someone and was in the area just a few miles away. She had travelled from somewhere near London.

I finally gave in and allowed for her to visit. I saw no harm in her visit. When she arrived, I welcomed her in, and we sat and talked for a while. It was rather awkward because she was not someone, I personally knew but I had heard of her through Tshidz. She asked a lot of questions about my situation with my in-laws and even asked why there were no pictures of Tshidz or any displayed in our living room. I found her really awkward and strange, but I didn't make much of it.

Days after her visit I was contacted by another Usher-girl who opted to give me free advice, she said she was a friend of Tshidz and wanted to warn me to be careful of these ladies from Usher and not to let them into my house.

She went on to tell me that there was a Facebook group or WhatsApp group on which these ladies were spreading gossip.

There was a callout to anyone who had any damning information about me to share, they were compiling a dossier at the request of my mother-in-law. (So, I was told).

She spoke of the things that their former head girl had posted on these social media platforms with regards her visit to my house.

Lessons in hindsight, I learnt a valuable lesson from this experience, indeed gossipers don't care about privacy, they don't care much about your grief, they come to find something to talk about. I witnessed this. It can be very disturbing at the time of morning when vicious and hurtful gossip is spread.

Don't confuse these gossipers who come disguised as friends with genuine caring friends. The gossip will aggressively seek information on the deceased and will not stop until every stone has been turned.

While it's fine for genuine friends to listen to the family of the deceased when they vent, prying is a different topic altogether.

Unfortunately, when one is grieving, they are vulnerable and so the alertness or awareness to spot those prying gossipers is almost non-existent.

Indeed, funerals are also highly personal occasions, they typically are wide open. Anyone and everyone who knew the deceased could come and pay their respects.

Ironically gossipers are usually those that know so little about you. I was labelled an abuser, there was even talk that Tshidz and I had divorced. I had moved out and the worst one which unfortunately was paddled by my in-laws was that I had gone to Russia and acquired Polonium 2-10 a deadly poison and I had used that to kill my wife. I can look back and laugh and joke about the outrageous and ridiculousness of some of these rumours now. But at the time these gossipers were cooking up and serving these fabrications it was extremely hurtful.

I was fortunate enough to have very supportive friends my circle of friends that I have known for all my adult life, people who were friends to both Tshidz and I.

Those were and are the people who knew the dynamics in our relationship. They knew my character and that of Tshidz. They stood by me and walked with me through these turbulent times.

I am forever, grateful for their undying love and care.

But it would be an incomplete story if I do not mention the close friends who became chancers and opportunists and fanned the flames of gossip for personal benefit.

One worth mentioning is one of Tshidz friend from Wolverhampton, this lady did the unthinkable she claimed that Tshidz had bought her a car and I was refusing to give it to her.

She got herself so close to my mother-in-law and a part of me believes that most of the misinformation that caused a further rift between my mother-in-law, and I was down to her engineering.

She unashamedly claimed that Tshidz was such a close friend to her, and she had bought a Jeep for her, and I was refusing to hand over the car.

In truth I had bought the jeep with the intention of sending it to Zimbabwe.

We had two cars but mostly used one reason being I work from home and Tshidz was the one who drove to work.

So, when her friend from Wolverhampton said she was looking for a car because her car had broken down. Tshidz being the kind person she was offered to lend her my car which was parked outside.

This was not the first time Tshidz had offered to help a friend in such a way she had previously done the same to another of her friends from the church we used to go to. Unfortunately, that friend racked the car, and it never came back.

And so, when it came to my Jeep, I refused to have it borrowed out to the Wolverhampton lady and that was her bone and beef with me.

Interestingly all this happened months before Tshidz died but she brought it up later with a twist her clam was the car was bought for her. Now she wanted the car gifted to my mother-in-law.

Gossipers and opportunistic chancers can compound grief and stress for those grieving. Indeed, dealing with family dysfunction after death is more difficult than dealing with it during ordinary circumstances because of elevated emotions. When a family is estranged, and a member of the family dies, things become a bit more complicated.

These opportunistic chances and their gossip loving cheerers are not interested in figuring out the best ways possible to bring the family closer together.

They want more divisions and more drama so they can find something to talk about or post in their WhatsApp group and others social media platforms.

A cousin (sister) of Tshidz set up a Facebook page and solicited funds she collected money into her account, some of my friends told me about this, but at the time I thought no harm or saw no ill intentions in this because I thought it would be accounted for and put to good use.

Her cousins came over to the house as soon as news of her death was announced initially, we all seemed to be working towards the same goals. They collected money from friends and well-wishers a traditional custom practiced in Zimbabwean societies. Those who came to pass their condolences contribute monies known in Shona as (chemwa) her cousin from Newcastle and the one from Wolverhampton collected this money. Nonetheless things shifted and for reasons known to them they withheld the money and never accounted for it.

One of my close friends and his wife who took on the responsibility of managing the funeral finances tried to get updates on the funds that had been raised but all their efforts to get an account from these cousins failed.

I told them not to worry and I provided all funds required to get things moving.

My mother-in-law was still cooperating at that stage and told my friend and his wife that the cousins would give an account later. But that never materialised.

While all this was taking place the cousin from Wolverhampton who was at the house rummaged through all documents in the house and took all insurance policy documents and birth certificate and to this day, she hasn't said what she did with them.

All she said was that my mother-in-law had need for them and she had asked her to get them.

I knew then that this was about Tshidz's estate, they had already started plotting.

I started hearing about the divorce rumours, a story had been cooked up that Tshidz and I had divorced. At first, I did not let it bother me because I knew it was a fabrication. However, it turned out that they had gone to extreme lengths even doctoring documents from Zimbabwe to validate that lie.

To avoid conflict, I decided to remove myself from anything to do with the administration of the estate. I left all of that to Tshidz's brother, he was one to receive anything that came from her work and anything that had to do with insurance claims.

I spoke to my son about it and told him what was going on.

They assured him that a trust fund would be set up and when he turns 18, they will give him what's his.

Like I said a part of me still believes some of the actions of my mother-in-law were influenced by the misinformation peddled by the gossipers. Her mistake was believing the opportunistic chancers.

All my efforts to reconcile at the time to allow for a befitting send off for Tshidz were snuffed. In the end I had to do what I had to do and that was to bury my wife. With or without them.

Even the traditional contributions made by friends (chemwa) was taken by these chancers.

Not a single penny was put to help with funeral costs, but all was diverted to God knows where?

I hold no grudge they came in caused disruption and confusion, but I thank God I held my own.

In the end I gave my wife a befitting send-off, my friends and her friends and work colleagues attended, and all went smoothly.

15

Preparing for the day of burial

There's a line in William Shakespeare's play Henry V, which cuts to the heart of preparedness: "All things are ready, if our mind be so." Readying your mind means strengthening it for what's ahead: all the people, sights, sounds and strong emotions of the day.

And so, preparations were made a date was set Tshidz was to be laid to rest at Wombridge cemetery in Telford.

I met with the Wombridge Parish vicar and went through the program. We consulted with the funeral directors, and all was in place.

Friends and family were notified and when the day came the funeral service was conducted and everything went to plan.

The in-laws boycotted but friends and colleagues joined my son and I to bid our final farewells to Tshidz.

The death of a loved one is among the most traumatic experiences one can ever endure. The early days of bereavement are a time of frayed nerves, when emotions run high, and hours of restful sleep are hard to find. These difficult days are then followed by the funeral service (where, even though you are grief stricken, you're expected to perform with some social grace). How can you possibly survive; or better yet thrive, during such trials as these?

Could there be anything more difficult than preparing for a funeral? Certainly, such an end-of-life event is hard to look forward to with any great enthusiasm. Worse still as a spouse far from close family. It was particularly difficult for me because I had relocated to the diaspora. I was miles away from Zimbabwe and didn't have any close family in England.

Indeed, I can attest; preparing for a funeral service takes time and forethought. Needless to say added stress and family conflicts only make an already difficult situation more stressful.

Almost a month after Tshidz had died we finally managed to bury her. There had been a tag of war between my mother-in-law and myself as to where and when she could be buried. Zimbabwe or England? In the end after much contestation the decision was mine to make and England it was.

Several uncles and aunties had popped up, all claiming to represent my mother-in-law and at some point, moves were made to contact the funeral directors and retrieve the body from the mortuary and transport it to Zimbabwe without my knowledge, nonetheless the clandestine moves failed.

With the help and support of a handful of my close friends I had to plan and prepare my wife's funeral. I found it baffling, terrifying, weird, overwhelming, devastating and incredibly important – a very bad mixture. I wanted to honour her with a dignified send off, I wanted it to go smoothly.

It all started with a trip to the funeral director – not someone I had on speed dial. I remember one of the bereavement team members at the hospital had given me the number of the local funeral directors. I suddenly remember that I had seen their offices not far from our house.

I remembered that years before while walking my son to school, I would walk or drive past the parlour thinking: "I'll never go there while I'm alive." Alas, I found myself walking in to sort out arrangements for my wife's funeral.

The meeting with the funeral director took a while, ticking off a number of decisions. Where do you want the service, what time should it be, how many cars, cremation or burial, pine or oak, chrome handles or gold-painted ones, live music or taped, will anyone be visiting the body, do you want the corpse to have makeup, etc – and I had to make a lot of decisions, but I also wanted my son to have a say in the type of coffin and how things would go on the day. I also had to make sure that I don't overwhelm him while making sure that his opinions and contributions were incorporated into the funeral arrangements.

It was important for me to talk to my son about funeral services before we attended it.

I had made it a point to include him in the planning to the extent possible. I ask him if there are things he would like to incorporate into the event or if there were special ways that he would like to honour his mother.

I spoke to him about what to expect before, during, and after the services, burial. This conversation included discussions about things like the body viewing, burial, and what types of emotions he may witness, what types of emotions he was likely to feel during all this.

We discussed his concerns and worries. I enquired if there were any parts of these rituals that worried him. We brainstormed ways for him to cope in the moment. He wrote down his speech because he wanted to say a few words at the church service, and he did an excellent job of it on the day.

He even became a pallbearer on the final walk to the grave. It was emotional, it was tough to watch him. But I was proud of his determination and courage in the whole process.

The day before the funeral we went and got some suits. My son had suggested that we have something yellow which was his mother's favourite colour. So, we had black suit and yellow neckties.

We had also asked friends and colleagues to have something yellow at the burial service.

I had spoken with the vicar prior to the day and arranged the readings, poems, music, and hymns that had special meaning not only to us but Tshidz. The vicar we used, and the church was not our regular church in fact we had never attended the Church of England but in the end, they gave us a very dignified and worthy service on that day.

I also made sure that there were opportunities for others to participate in the speeches and music.

One of her friends and colleagues from work Shelly spoke and our family friends Stephanie and Sarah shared eulogies and some very comforting words.

Her other friends from previous churches and school helped as pallbearers and ushers during the church service.

16

My advice to friends when you learn of someone's loss

When someone you care about is grieving after a loss, it can be difficult to know what to say or do. The bereaved struggle with many intense and painful emotions, including depression, anger, guilt, and profound sadness. Often, they also feel isolated and alone in their grief since the intense pain and difficult emotions can make people uncomfortable about offering support.

You may be afraid of intruding, saying the wrong thing, or making your loved one feel even worse at such a difficult time. Or maybe you think there's little you can do to make things better. That's understandable. But don't let discomfort prevent you from reaching out to someone who is grieving. Now, more than ever, your loved one needs your support. There is a difference between Support and comfort. We make the mistake of not knowing how to help someone grieving.

You may think I am splitting hairs here but hear me out. Although support and comfort may sound similar, in this context, the ideas of 'comforting' and 'supporting' have two very different implications. A look at the dictionary definitions of the two will help elucidate.

Comfort: (*noun*) a state of physical ease and freedom from pain or constraint. (*verb*) make (someone) feel less unhappy, console.

Support: (*verb*) bear all or part of the weight of; hold up. (*verb*) give assistance to. (*noun*) the action of bearing the weight of something or someone or of being so supported. (*noun*) material assistance, i.e., emotional help offered to someone in distress, approval, and encouragement.

There is a clear difference 'Comfort' implies a desire to free someone from their pain and make them feel less unhappy, while 'support' means a willingness to provide assistance and help.

Most of us have probably gotten good at the comforting others, thus when we approach someone who is grieving, our first inclination may be to fall back on words of optimism. The natural thing for us is to try to take away their pain and so we find ourselves saying things that look for a silver lining and which begin with "at least" and at times end with "I know you are strong". Platitudes, "be strong", and inspiring statements may be well intentioned, but they often minimize the gravity of a person's loss and make it seem as though you either don't care or aren't paying attention to the reality that is standing right in front of you.

My Christian friends were the worst at confusing comfort with support. Prior to this experience I probably would have done the same. Flood, the grieving person with philosophical expression and clichés. The tendency to shower a griever with scriptural verses is almost like a favourite go to, for most Christians. I am by no means saying it is wrong, but from my experience with grieving, all these so-called uplifting scriptures become banalities at some point in your grieving process.

I remember talking to a close friend who had lost their mother at about the same time that my wife had died. She spoke about how irritated she was by people who would say "it is well" her question was what is well about my situation and my loss?

Instead of attempting to comfort the person who is grieving, my suggestion would be to try focusing on what you can do to help support them in moving forward through the pain. Take it easy on the platitudes.

Most of us already have a natural inclination to support others and as such we have the tools to make us great grief supporters.

To be a good grief supporter one has to be willing and able to:

Show genuine caring and compassion: No one knows the perfect thing to say, so stop stressing. Instead, focus on treating the griever with caring and compassion. Sometimes this is as simple as asking how the person is doing and then actually listening to what they have to say.

Provide concrete assistance: It's tempting to ask the griever to let you know what they need, but it's far more useful to offer specific help. Consider a list of things you can do. Hopefully, you know the griever well enough to predict a few of their needs.

Actively listen: Talking to someone who will simply listen is often precisely what a griever needs. You may feel like you need to provide answers, but usually just having the opportunity to talk things out can help someone organize their thoughts and feelings. Besides, the conclusions they reach on their own are far more valuable than any given to them.

Be present: Without hovering, be available to the griever by letting them know they can call at any time or by casually check in once in a while. Don't push and don't pressure. If they don't want to talk and if they don't take you up on your offers, that's okay. Also, grievers will still be hurting months, even years after a death, well after the casseroles and messages of concern stop rolling in. For this reason, the check-in's that happen after they have mostly been left alone will send the message that you understand their pain is enduring and reminds them you will be there for them in the long-term. Make it casual, send a card or an e-mail; that way they can choose not to respond if they don't feel like talking. Don't take it to heart if you don't get a response and follow their cues. If they don't engage with you, it's probably wise to give them a little space.

But the bereaved need to feel that their loss is acknowledged, it's not too terrible to talk about, and their loved one won't be forgotten. One day they may want to cry on your shoulder, on another day they may want to vent, or sit in silence, or share memories. By being present and listening compassionately, you can take your cues from the grieving person. Simply being there and listening to them can be a huge source of comfort and healing.

GET IN TOUCH

As soon as you learn about the death, phone, visit or write to the person's friends or relatives. If you live nearby, you might be able to offer some practical help like collecting a pension, taking the children to school or doing the ironing. There is often the assumption that family grief is private and that you may be intruding. But many people live far away from their family and would appreciate your help.

FINDING THE RIGHT WORDS

Don't stay away because you don't know what to say. The fact that you are there is enough. A warm handshake or an arm around their shoulder can mean so much to someone who feels isolated and lonely.

AFTER THE FUNERAL

Being there for a friend after the funeral is very important. They may want to talk about the person they have lost, and this is probably the most important part of the grieving process. Listen with care and attention. This may be painful for you both but by going over the final period of the deceased's life together, they will start to accept what has happened. Small details of what happened in the last days before the death become terribly important.

VISITING

If you visit, you can help with practical jobs like housework or preparing a meal. People who have lost a loved one often don't have the energy to do this. It's a good idea to be specific in what you can help with but be careful not to take over or do anything without permission.

BE SENSITIVE

Try not to show your own grief. Don't say, 'I know how you must be feeling.' You cannot begin to know how they feel, and we all have our own story when it happens to us. Don't make comparisons or judgements. It might have been worse for someone else, but that will not help your friend. Some people like to be held, whereas others feel it is an invasion of their privacy. Some people may want to talk, whereas others may want to sit in silence. Explain you are happy to be with them for as long as they want.

Make it clear to them that you are not embarrassed if they cry. Reassure them that this is a perfectly normal reaction. Be patient and understanding. One of the best ways to help your friend is to allow them to feel what they want to feel. They may feel anger (which may be directed at you but is not personal), guilt or fear. Let them talk these feelings through with you – don't try to stop them because you think they are irrational.

THE FUTURE

Having a social life can be difficult for people who have lost a loved one. You can help by inviting them to join you in social events or encouraging them to follow other interests such as evening classes – you could go to one together. Christmas is a particularly bad time. If they won't be seeing their family, perhaps you could invite them to join you on Christmas Day or Boxing Day. At the very least, spare the time to drop by with a cheerful word and a small gift.

The most important thing you can give to your friend is to be yourself and to be there for them.

17

Life goes on; grieving changes the way you view the world

It is important to understand and know that when you are grieving people you care about, friends and colleagues continue with their lives as normal.

Those around you may empathise and sympathise with you. Indeed, they may understand that you are grieving but their lives continue as normal. They still must work, party, laugh and concentrate on their jobs.

I personally had moments when I found it difficult to focus and concentrate on things that needed to be done. I found it hard to focus on my work. In fact, it took me almost two years to bounce back into rhythm with regards work.

I can't emphasise this point enough. It is important to note that even in the deepest moments of grieving the world goes on. Even when you are half insane from grief, bills still need to be paid; even when you feel like you swallowed a hand grenade, you still must balance the cheque book.

Thus, it goes without saying that one must try to focus and concentrate on work and getting the bills paid and keeping the household moving even when arrested by grieving.

Undeniably it's hard when you have always been a focused, fabulous, functional person. But grief is the worst, and it really messes with your brain. I had to come to an understanding of this during my grieving. I had to self-motivate, I had to and still make uplifting self-declarations and manifest that I am not a failure for being distracted. I am a normal, wonderful, griever who is just doing my best to cope. So, my humble advice to those going through grieving is that in those moments when you have lost all focus, try to give yourself some permission and space to know it's okay. You are still a fabulous person… And it might just take some time and a little work to get that focus back.

Grief and concentration don't mix well.

That is not a sign that you are losing it, I can attest to that. Struggling to concentrate is very normal soon after a loss. It is simply a sign that your brain is completely consumed by something painful, overwhelming, and life changing.

That said, if the inability to focus keeps up for an extended period of time or is interfering with your life in an unmanageable way for example if you're at risk of losing your job, you can't care for your children, etc., then I suggest you seek professional help from a therapist if that is an available option or talk to a trusted friend never be ashamed to get help. I found that there are friends and family members who are always equipped with some basic tips and tools that may probably help you over the hurdle.

Though I certainly don't believe time heals all wounds, I do know that time helps a lot with regards to grief and concentration. It takes time for your brain to adjust to a new reality, to the completely different world that exists after your loss. There are conflicting emotions to process, fears and anxieties to cope with, secondary losses to navigate, and countless other things your brain is trying to manage … but that does get easier with time.

I came across an interesting theory called the theory of shattered assumptions.

This is in a book by psychologist Ronnie Janoff-Bulman she described the theory of shattered assumptions in her book, Shattered Assumptions: Towards a New Psychology of Trauma. Although this theory is most often applied to trauma (which many have probably experienced), it helps to explain adjustment after any type of experience that challenges a person's belief system or worldview.

In a very basic nutshell, the theory of shattered assumptions says that people operate according to a conceptual system based on a set of assumptions about the world, the self, and others. These personally held assumptions about how the world works help you make sense of the world and your role within it. They also help you to feel safe, capable, and in control of what happens to you and, in some ways, those around you. Psychologists refer to our basic assumptions as the "assumptive world" and believe that, when extreme events challenge this assumptive world, significant distress and disruption can occur.

To use a personal example: Before Tshidz got diagnosed with cancer my life was great, the world was good. My assumptions of the world and life led me to assume that the world is logical – that bad things happen for a reason; there is justice in the world; and if you 'do everything right,' then things will turn out okay. After death, I realised that there are things my worldview absolutely cannot reconcile or account for.

In the theory of shattered assumptions, Janoff-Bulman discusses three main assumptions that can be challenged by trauma. You may have experienced upheaval around one or more of these basic assumptions, depending on your previously held beliefs, your perceptions around your loved one's death, and your grief.

Assumptions About the Benevolence of the World:

These assumptions refer to beliefs that:

1. The world is generally a safe place where more good happens than bad, and
2. That most people have good intentions and can be trusted.

Together, these beliefs can lead a person to underestimate the likelihood that negative events will happen to them and create a false sense of invulnerability. When a traumatic event shatters these assumptions, a person can feel anxious and helpless in a world that suddenly seems threatening and filled with dangerous and bad people.

My immediate experience after Tshidz's death left me feeling exactly that, friends that she had trusted suddenly became dangerous and bad people that I couldn't trust.

How you feel about the benevolence of the world in the wake of your loved one's death may depend on how you perceive the events that led up to and followed their death. In general, once you experience the death of a loved one, it becomes increasingly difficult to ignore the reality that your loved ones can be taken from you at any moment.

The other assumptions we hold are about the meaningfulness of the world.

These assumptions refer to beliefs that the world is orderly, just, and logical. In other words, this is the belief that the world makes sense.

I fell into that category. I had always held the assumption that "Everything happens for a reason," thus, I correspondingly believed that I had more control over events than I truly did.

I assumed we (I) live in a "just world," I believed that I could protect myself from negative experiences by behaving in a way that is "right" or "good."

I believed that: If we eat right and exercise, we won't get cancer. If I'm a good father, my child won't use drugs or engage in risky behaviour. If I was strong in my faith, I would be protected from evil.

Nonetheless, Tshidz's death taught me something. It made me view things differently.

Indeed, your loved one's death may contradict many of your beliefs about the meaningfulness of the world. Perhaps the death feels unfair, perhaps it violates your sense of control, or perhaps it proves that bad things can happen to good people. Again, I can attest to that.

18

Finding love after bereavement

As humans we have an unlimited capacity for love. What curtails our ability to love are the conditions we place on loving.

A classic quote said to be from Carter Crocket which most people attribute to A.A. Milne, the author of the Winnie-the-Pooh books, as the words of Christopher Robin to his best friend Winnie-the-Pooh.

Somehow succinctly sums up what I am trying to put across.

> *"If ever there is tomorrow when we're not together... there is something you must always remember. You are braver than you believe, stronger than you seem, and smarter than you think. But the most important thing is, even if we're apart... I'll always be with you"*

Life can be lonely and difficult after a bereavement. Adjusting to life as a single parent I had times that I struggled to cope. There was no-one to talk to about day-to-day issues and all the household tasks that fell upon my shoulders. My son and I were both grieving and at most times there was little support. A part of me longed to have someone to love again. But as someone who had lost a partner to death, I was very hesitant about entering into a new relationship. I was not sure if I would be able to handle another loss. For a while after Tshidz died I was afraid to truly love anyone. I had anxiety about letting someone get too close or falling in love with them in case I lost them too. I know this might sound silly, but it really was how I felt.

The reality of looking for love again after losing your soulmate can be terrifying and confusing. You might feel guilty, like you're betraying the person you lost. You might worry what your friends and family members will think. And then there's the question of how soon you start dating again? When do you even know you're ready?

There is no doubt that grief is tough. But it makes you strong. We humans are very resilient, and in addition to that, we have an unlimited capacity for love.

The big question is how soon after the loss of a beloved partner should someone start a new relationship?

My honest answer would be no-one plans these things. It often just happens that you are lucky enough to meet someone with whom you can bond with and get alone with. Someone who understands your story and situation.

I speak about Tshidz a lot she was in my life almost every day of my adult life.

Admittedly, the love you have for someone who dies is often idealised and strengthened after their death. When we lose someone, we tend to remember only the good things about them, which makes it pretty difficult for any new relationship to live up to the memories of the partner you lost.

It's inevitable that comparisons will be made, and perhaps the new love doesn't seem as strong as the old relationship.

All relationships are different. When we are grieving, we are in turmoil and experience a roller coaster of emotions. Your new relationship will be different. It is another person in another time, with different life experiences. You haven't known them as long and need time to get used to one another.

So, my advice from experience would be:

Give it time. Try not to judge them by the same criteria as

your previous relationship.

Accept their love and support and take it slowly.

If you are lucky enough to find someone who cares for you, then don't be afraid to build on that relationship. Share and talk to your family and friends so that they understand.

It is your life. Take up the challenge and have the confidence to build a new relationship. You might be one of the lucky ones, who have not one, but two great loves in their life.

Don't rush, don't let societal pressure push you into a relationship before you are ready and don't let gossipers deter or put you off getting into a relationship. Do it when the time is right.

You will know when the time is right. My advice would be let yourself be guided by your inner feelings.

There is pressure from society particularly our Zimbabwean culture to rush you into a relationship. The general belief and argument from our society particularly for widowers is that you need to find someone who can support you and your children. Or the classic (every man needs a woman).

Indeed, finding someone who can support you and your children at this difficult time is a bonus. Nonetheless, it should not be rushed. Allow yourself space to grieve and regroup your thoughts and allow things to progress organically and don't respond to societal pressure.

Some people are lucky enough to meet loving, caring, and supportive people during their first year of bereavement and get happily married to their new partners. For others it takes a while. Others choose never to marry again.

Society seems to judge widows more harshly than widowers in this circumstance and there are so many tales in history of evil widows preying on men or of women who fell in love very soon after losing their husbands and were heavily criticised. (We have all heard of those stories where it's said the body of the deceased had not even gone cold and the widow or widower was already marrying someone else) society exaggerates these tales without consideration of how that can impact on a person's ability to move on and find love.

It is common to experience judgement and opposition from relatives and friends when a new relationship starts soon after a bereavement, but it is not for them to judge. It doesn't mean that you loved the deceased person any less. It can help to talk openly to those who have doubts and explain that it doesn't mean that you don't love the person you have lost, but that you are honouring them by going on with your life and looking for happiness again. You will always treasure the memories you had but you cannot be miserable for ever and they wouldn't have wanted you to be.

There is no time limit for grief, and because you re-marry or start a new relationship does not mean that you have forgotten your first love. You can love again.

It may be that family and friends take the news of a new relationship badly, especially close family members of the lost loved one. They may feel that their son or daughter is forgotten or given no respect. Their grief is still raw, and they can't understand how their son or daughter-in-law could do this. Children may be upset if their mother or father re-marries. You hear stories of sons or daughters complaining that the new partner is only after their mother or father's money.

But grief is not a competition. We don't have to prove to anyone how much we are grieving.

When we have lost someone, they would not have wanted us to be unhappy and alone for the rest of our lives. Our loved ones would have wanted us to find someone to love. It is fortunate when we meet someone early in our grief journey. It is better for children too, as they will experience their parent being happier and feel part of a family again.

In my experience men are more likely to marry again quite quickly after the loss of their wives than women do. Family focused men who have lost their wives can feel totally devastated. Their work life, home and children were their whole lives, and they find it difficult to function without a family around them. Their marriage or relationship form an essential part of their identity.

In the end, we all experience love and grief in our own individual ways, and there is no right or wrong way to cope with loss. We should all be open minded and supportive to those who have lost a loved one and be understanding when they find love again. Grief is not a competition. We don't have to prove how much we loved someone by how much we are miserable when they pass. I believe that making the most of life and moving on is a good way to honour our lost loved ones.

She Lived She Loved

A beautiful life we shared,
Tears of joy
Smiles in pain
Walks in the rain
Happiness with no refrain
You bulldozed like a train
though you were in pain
Travis and I shed tears when to eternity you were gone.
Your body interred, ashes to ashes
Dust to dust
The vicar prayed
Today we smile as we remember your love
Our hearts filled with memories that with us you shared
we celebrate your love, your legacy
with us you lived
You loved us to the end

Your happy memories forever we hold, the places we toured
The stories you told
Forever we will hold
The picture of your purest smile
Always expressed
Atop the Wrekin each time at the summit you smiled
Closed your eyes and you would pray
That one day you would fly

Your day came 29 May
and from your pain you flew away

Today like our Guardian angel you hoover above
watching over us
we smile
With our eyes open we see all that you have left for us,
happy memories indeed, inspiration and life's teachings
Yours was a good innings, you lived you loved

We cried, we grieved,
Saddened by family and dear ones who like vultures came
they spoke ill they took everything,
we dried our eyes rolled up our Sleeves
got on with the grind, like you would have advised
smile, open your eyes, love, and go on.
Thank you, Tshidzani Tshihamba Pongo (MaMoyo),
you lived you,
You loved
We walk with you
we love you

Two years on

From Brill &Trav
Rest easy, you lived you loved us to the end.

Lightning Source UK Ltd.
Milton Keynes UK
UKHW041328180722
406016UK00003B/828